Home and Other Places

Home and Other Places: Voices of Southwest Michigan is funded, in part, by a grant from the Michigan Council of Arts and Cultural Affairs. Additional support for the work of the Rural Voices, Country Schools team comes from Writing for the Challenge, an initiative of the National Writing Project Corporation that is supported by the Annenberg Rural Challenge.

The Third Coast Writing Project, directed by Dr. Ellen Brinkley of the Department of English of Western Michigan University, is a teachers-teaching-teachers program that provides services to southwest Michigan teachers and school districts without regard to race, color, religion, age, sex, or handicap.

The views expressed in this book do not necessarily represent those of the funding organizations or of Western Michigan University.

michigan council for
arts and cultural affairs

Home and Other Places
Voices of Southwest Michigan

Edited by

Sherrie Britton

Renee Callies

Pen Campbell

Dan Holt

New Issues Press
College of Arts and Sciences

WESTERN MICHIGAN UNIVERSITY

Kalamazoo, Michigan – 1998

Kalamazoo, Michigan 1998
ISBN 0-932826-73-3

Additional copies may be ordered for $5.00 plus $2.00 for shipping and handling. Check or money order should accompany order and be sent to

New Issues Press
Western Michigan University – Walwood Hall
1201 Oliver Street
Kalamazoo, Michigan 49008-3801

Cover Design – Linda K. Judy

Typesetting – Cindy Jo Schnotala

Page Layout and Design – Bill Hamilton

Cover photos courtesy of   Pen Campbell (front)
                             John Campbell (back)

Printed in the United Sates of America

Contents

Introduction
Confessions of a Small Town Writer

I'll be turning 50 in a few weeks. And I've been thinking about it . . . a lot.

Five decades seems like such a long time. Growing up, I distinctly remember saying to a friend that people 50 years old were **really** old, too old to have fun. And I never thought that I would live that long, and I never thought that I would live that long in just one place. But I have.

For 50 years, with the exception of two years teaching in Illinois, I have lived in Southwestern Michigan. I grew up just north of St. Joe, attended grade school and high school there, and went off to college just an hour's drive away in Kalamazoo. For the past 26 years, I've been teaching in the same high school I graduated from in '66.

Living and working in one place as I have for so long has its benefits: I know all the shortcuts, the best fishing holes, and the best barbers. I also don't have any trouble cashing a check in town, and I have an assigned seat at the local McDonald's where I often eat breakfast with guys I've known since grade school. I am presently teaching the children of former students and will soon be teaching the grandchildren of kids I went to school with. There is a feeling of community here that I could not get anyplace else because I have grown into this place much as lichen grows into rock; I have become part of the rock that is my home town.

As a writer, I am just beginning to understand the power of community: I am just beginning to understand this town and its people. I know, for example, because I have lived here so long, that beneath the relatively new video store are layers of other businesses, including the Big Ben Drive-in where I used to spend extra money and time trying to impress a particular carhop. I can say to my children, this is the spot where I first saw your mother. And I can say, right there is the spot where Chester, a local character, jumped into the river and was never seen again, because I was there, or at least I knew people who were there.

I am part of the big blizzards of '67 and '73, and the summer storm that knocked down many of the trees on the bluff in the mid 80s. I am part of the little league tournaments and countless Friday night football games under the lights, in which it is not unusual for this town where fewer than 10,000 people live for nearly 5,000 of them to be in attendance. This is the place from which I get my inspiration and the images with which I fill my poetry.

So I guess, this is a confession of sorts. I am officially a small town writer, as well as a teacher, former little league coach, current fisherman, etc., etc. I make this confession freely. I think now that it is a fine thing to turn 50 in a place that I know so well, and I think it is a fine thing to write about that place and the people who live there.

And apparently others feel as I do because this volume is filled with their voices about home towns and rural places in Southwestern Michigan and the people who live there. The voices in this book come from small children and senior citizens, from teachers and nurses, from college students and business executives, from high school students working part time and from stay-at-home mothers who work all the time. In all, over 400 Southwestern Michigan residents submitted over 1,000 poems and short prose works for this book. We ended up choosing, with great difficulty, 104 pieces from 91 writers for final publication.

We wish we could have chosen more, but we think we have chosen well.

Dan Holt

Editors' Note:

The poems and short prose pieces included in this collection were edited with care to preserve the authentic voices. You may find that if you read the pieces in the order presented, they fit together like a patchwork quilt—the overlapping stories creating an image of Southwestern Michigan.

Turning 50

Dan Holt

Sometimes Poetry comes to me
like a crow in a Wallace Stevens' field
or falls like the doe from Stafford's River Road
or tempts me like plums cold and sweet on a plate
in Carlos's ice box.

Sometimes

But increasingly now
since I have found this age
I realize
Poetry
is living secretly
in a house my father built
hiding from me
like a child, half crazed
with delight
holding his hands over his
eyes, standing in the hall
closet, crouched in a clothes hamper, or wedged
between the dryer and water
heater.

I know this now that I am 50
that Poetry waits for me
in a place I know
well.

Sometimes he's asleep in a hayloft
above a stamping quarter horse
still steaming from a winter run
or fishing for crayfish
on the sun side of a slow summer river.

Insecurities of a Product of the Manufactured World

Rebecca Kosick

Why write without the knowledge to do so?
Maybe if I floated long enough
that my skin dissolved into the lake,
and I became part of it,
crashing on the nearby shore,
reflecting the blue of the air above me,
and delighting ten year olds as they ride my white-capped soul
all the way in.
Maybe then,
I would have something of importance to say.

Or perhaps
if the wind picked me up
from this four-walled room I haven't left all day
and tossed me into the clouds
so that I could fall upon the weddings
and the children's birthday parties,
and swell the earth so the farmers will dance among my drops, and praise
me for the couple bucks they earned today.
Perhaps then I would know enough to write something of worth.

Why can't I travel
until the earth that holds me is gone
and I fall 167 feet to find it,
only to create a beauty I never intended,
but that surpasses all else?
Why can't I be amazing enough
that people gain national recognition for hopping in a barrel
and falling with me
to the calm pool below?

I wish I could become the river
and make its turns,
and feel as the creatures inhabiting it

are torn through my skin
to be stuffed and mounted on a wall.
I wish I could be the river
until I'd seen the seasons change above me
enough times that I would be able to forgive,
even before the antifreeze joined my winding quest.

But instead,
I'm sitting here,
in artificially colored, created, and manufactured clothes
listening to a black-boxed, one woman band,
and about to be cleaned by water dripping from a pipe,
hoping one day I'll surround myself
with nature long enough that I'll know
two percent of what it knows
and be a genius.

St. Joseph High School

The Writer's Tools

Katherine E. Kendall

Rivers of many colors
flowing over a land of white
smooth, rolling, fluid

Soft crumbling line of yellow
on a green wall
brush it away
put it on again
dust floating in the air

Quick jerky scratches
drab gray lines
dull tip
irritated fingers
dry dead stick of wood

Centreville High School

Two Hawks

Matt O'Leary

Above the tree, two hawks circle aimlessly,
While below I try to compose a simile.
Around and around, they drift above me,
Like random thoughts strung together poetically.

One hawk spots a movement with his eye,
Like an arrow he makes his dive.
What it did to me I cannot say,
But all my poems left me when he glided away.

I wish my mind was like these awesome birds,
A predator that snatches up words.

Mattawan High School

A Tree Story

E. Blair Laing

Many, many years ago on May 7, on the outskirts of Eau Claire, Michigan on a bright and sunny day, a forest was being cut down by Farmer Brown. He wanted to grow corn and wheat.

The lumbermen stopped when they saw an itsy, bitsy evergreen tree. The tree was the size of a little bush. They asked Farmer Brown if they should chop it down. There was silence. A blue bird's chirp broke the silence. "Leave it!" yelled Farmer Brown over the howl of a wolf. "It may be of use."

So the lumbermen continued their work, leaving the tiny little evergreen tree.

The farmer decorated it with red, orange, yellow, green, pink, and purple Christmas lights that Christmas. It was brilliant.

In the summer, because it was a little taller and darker shade of green, it stood out very well. When they picked the corn, the tractors carefully went around the cute tree.

Soon it was taller than Farmer Brown's house. It was the most beautiful tree he had ever seen.

Over the years he grew to like the tree more and more and more.

One cold and windy winter day, the tree was blown down. The farmer was very sad. The next day he noticed a large tree in its place. It was pale green with frost.

The farmer didn't know that because he had treated the tree so well, that the Power of Nature had replaced the fallen tree with the "Wizard Tree," which is a tree that lives forever. It was always the most gorgeous tree in the land. People came from miles and miles away to see the frosty and sparkling "Wizard Tree." It was like a star. At night you could see it from the other side of Eau Claire. It was a beautiful sight.

Sometime you should visit the farms of Eau Claire out near Dowagiac. You might see the "Wizard Tree" although it's not small anymore. It still glistens with brightness when it is decorated with colors.

To the Brown School library.

Brown Elementary School

Blair Laing

Pine Trees

Katrina Tefft

Pine Trees smell like mints and
sound like the wind.
Pine trees taste like nasty alcohol (maybe)
and
Feel like needles.
They look like upside-down ties.

Colon Elementary School

Sarett Nature Center, New Year's Day '98

Ian Rastall

We need these quiet times, in these uncivilized sanctuaries, to replace our spirits, so drained away by the machinery of the social world. Something that before was insignificant, like one brown leaf, curled and hanging off a bare branch, can force the air into our lungs when the modern world has knocked the wind out of us.

I don't wonder what to say to Dave when we're out here. The genuine exertion of hiking this trail has turned off the cycling and recycling of thoughts in my head. In the car it was different. We passed the Baptist church on Main Street and I said to him, "There used to be a crack house down there." He said nothing. I tried to laugh it off: "That's changing the subject!" He pretended he hadn't heard what I said, and I said to him, "Never mind." Pretending not to hear is how people inside the Real will give us a second chance. But I was scared to know that there were in fact wrong things that I could say.

I stop on the trail to point out some animal tracks to Dave. I ask him if a deer could recognize a human footprint. He nods his head with wonder. "Yeah, maybe." We imagine a buck checking out the trails and saying, "Whoever made that track I'm staying away from him." We know we only half belong here. I stare down at my print, and can read "Skechers" stamped in backwards. Is this what we have, that somehow distinguishes us?

These thoughts can not be shared. What do you say to someone who is Real? You say nothing unless you have to, and keep the day on the ground.

He leaves me to myself, and I leave him to himself, and the two of us crunch down the snow in the weird beauty of living.

Hickory Creek Swamp

Ann Louise Williamson

It is April but the sun
feels old. He doses
himself with vapors
from the swamp. Last
night he set the clock
and went to bed early,
but this morning
he's muddled from
daylight-savings time
and sits with his neck-
scarf over his head.

Red-winged blackbirds
skim over the mist,
they flit from cattail
to grass-top, flashing
theatrical red hearts
on their sleeves.
The crow who wintered
here all winter
watches these foolish
newcomers, crow-black
as himself. So once
in the Old World
a Neanderthal stood
watching bands of
prettily-wristed sapiens
gathering in the valley.
And the sun smiled
with his young face
upon the mists of April.

My Own World

Catherine Stasevich

A few of my friends and I have a place back in my woods called Cheetah Ville. Cheetah Ville has come a long way since third grade (we were really into cheetahs back then) when there were three houses, and tiny little gardens with nothing in them but violets and crab grass.

Now we have *real* houses made out of logs and sticks, tied together with baling twine, instead of just having twigs balance against each other. We also have large gardens (and small ones) with hostas, impatiens, pansies, bulbs, lily of the valley, and anything else we can get! In addition, we also have an entry garden and a small pond lined all the way around with gardens (the pond, by the way, is a major upgrade from the scummy shower curtain we *used* to have).

To get to Cheetah Ville, you walk up a windy, curvy, hosta lined path and through our forked tree entrance. The first garden, on your right, is obviously the entry garden. There are giant bleeding heart seedlings on the left.

The first house you get to is mine. You walk between the gardens lining my path and past my twin triangular gardens at the door. Once you enter my house, directly on the right is my sitting room, the first part of my trellis house. In front is my kitchen. If you go left from there, you are at my patio. There is a tree there encircled by small flowering plants with many tree pots. To the right and front is my herb garden that has lots of chives in it. Around my patio are also most of my plants that can't tolerate dense shade.

From the end of my path you go towards the pond and pass my large garden on the way. On either side of the pond is my sister, Karen's, garden, and my friend, Molly's.

Past the pond and directly to the left is Molly's house (in front is Karen's friend, Christina's, but since she's so new, it isn't much yet). Directly on the right when you enter Molly's house is her kitchen, on the left is a small part of her garden, and in front is her sitting room. If you go to the left, you are on Molly's path with gardens to the left.

At the end of Molly's path you are at the beginning of Karen's extremely long path. Her house really isn't much to look at yet, since it's so new, but it is by far the roomiest house in Cheetah Ville!

As you have probably guessed, we have four members in Cheetah Ville: myself, Karen, Christina, and Molly. We all have specific jobs in Cheetah Ville, except Christina, since she's so new.

I am the main gardener and caretaker, meaning I water the gardens and hanging pots, and take care of the rest of Cheetah Ville. Karen is the herbalist. She has the main store of herbs, such as chives, and what we call salad plants. Molly is our architect. She has built all the buildings in Cheetah Ville, and in addition, has made up our alphabet and name symbols. She has also thought up our ceremonies, which are becoming a major part of Cheetah Ville.

Through Cheetah Ville we are learning problem solving by figuring out how to best build things. Through the years we have learned *not* to build our houses on just one tree, or to make the sticks do balancing acts for supports. We have learned a lot of landscaping techniques through Cheetah Ville, and I believe, skills for life. I don't think any of us members will ever forget our own world.

Gull Lake Middle School

Weeds

Kitty Wunderlin

Elegant, hybrid, Gloriosa daisies danced in the breeze. Beside them Foxgloves leaned and shyly regarded their reflection in the dark water of the goldfish pool. A one-of-a-kind rose served as hostess for this summer garden party. The weeds stood all around the farm's lawn. Queen Anne's Lace, Clover, Yarrow, Common Asters and Day-Lilies looking in through the rusty squares of old wire fence, taunting the fancy garden club flowers and threatening to poke through and shake their seeds. The summer-sun laughed through the leaves of one hundred-year-old sugar maples.

It was the first Monday of the month and Aunt Gertrude finished her chores early. This was the day that the Garden Club met.

She poured water from the teakettle into a metal dishpan and went into the pantry to wash up. Her just pressed, light blue and white print dress, with the lace collar and glass buttons, hung from the top of the door. Her wide brim, white straw hat and matching purse and shoes waited on the bed. Her big straw garden hat, muddy boots and apron all hung on hooks in the back room taking the afternoon off.

Now in her little back bedroom, she carefully brushed her long gray-white hair, wrapping it into a bun with a twist and a pin that her strong arms and hands had perfected. She didn't really need to look in the mirror of the old dresser to do this. She patted cornstarch on her face. She prided herself on her white skin and went to great lengths not to let the sun touch it.

She now stooped to put the finishing touches on her six-foot "Ma Kettle" frame because standing straight up in the little room did not allow for her head to be seen in the mirror. She smoothed her hair, adjusted her collar and straightened the material around a button. She was ready. She picked up her purse and took one last look. She liked how she looked and felt.

Her two-inch heels clacked on the old, uneven, linoleum floor. Everything was neat and in its place. The table was set for dinner. Lester would not have to wait to eat. The back screen door banged shut behind her. She saw Uncle Lester coming up the lane.

He was "Pa Kettle" skinny. Tiny, spry and very strong, he often looked as though he would dance a jig and his smile told you ahead of time, that his words would be dry and understated. There were darkened places on his suspenders where he hung his thumbs before snapping the suspenders for punctuation. In his arms was a tremendous bouquet of Queen Anne's Lace, Clover, Day-Lilies, Yarrow, Butterfly Weed, and Aster.

"Lester," her voice celebrated his name with, what they call on the farm, a holler.

"Gertrude, what do you see?" he called from behind the bouquet. He was already laughing with delight. Partly from seeing her look so beautiful and partly because he had a joke tucked in his whole being.

She loved him and always made his moments sweeter. She hollered back to him, "I see a huge bundle of weeds with legs, coming up the lane into my yard. Weed seeds jumpin' this way and that, with every step."

"Do you have a vase?" he teased.

"Lester Goodspeed! You get those weeds out of here!" she commanded as she headed for the barn to get the Old Ford out.

"Don't you want to take these to the Garden Club?" he giggled. He was now shaking with laughter.

She started the Old Ford and shot out of the barn. There was only one, pedal-to-the-floor speed, when Aunt Gertrude was at the wheel. Lester watched the dust roll up behind her as she headed to town. He pumped some water into a bucket, arranging the weeds carefully, and then carried them inside, placing them right in the middle of the huge dining room table. Now he savored the delicious joy of what she would say when she got home and saw them there.

Pickles

Kristin Kelly

she asks me about school while we
sit on the davenport and stir our ice cream.
"fine" i say as i am more interested
in what occupies the afternoon of
a seventy year old flower, bright as her
first spring bloom.
"i did the warsh and hung it up so it will
smell like the sun," she says.
that same smell follows her into the
kitchen as we make salads to go
with supper. "pickles ?" she asks.
and i nod. she always calls cucumbers "pickles."
"i still have the beethoven cd you loaned me, she says.
"good dinner music," i think out loud. And she has me remind her of how to
     use her new "boom box."
we light candles for dinner and call grandpa.
i hit the lights on my way to the kitchen to get the milk
gramma makes me drink.
"kin hardly see yer plate," says grampa.
"but it's more romantic this way grampa," i say.
and gramma nods.
"might as well go eat on the davenport where 'least i kin see," says grampa.
he always calls the sofa "davenport."

St. Joseph High School

Talking Hands

Scott Peterson

My grandmother lived to be 92 years old and I can't remember one word she
  ever said.
Not a "Job worth doing is worth doing right," or "Good fences make good
  neighbors,"
not even a "Look both ways before you cross the road."

But I do remember how the rows of crops spread out around her house like
  rings in water,
as if dropped in a pond of green corn.
And the leafy trees and cool shade that covered her house on summer
  afternoons;
the high ceilings and dark wood that trimmed her doorways and walls;
and the pink rainbows that danced on her carpet as the evening light
passed through the leaded glass windows in her parlor.

I remember getting mail out of a little wooden box with a window in front at
  the general store in town;
my first cup of fresh perked coffee served in a thin white cup and saucer at her
  oak table with the claw feet;
playing battle ships on the old farm implements parked in the vacant fields like
  rusty dinosaurs;
sitting in the balcony of the Lutheran church, looking down at the bald, shiny
  heads and sunburned necks;
going down to the town dump to shoot rats and blast apart empty mayonnaise
  jars;
and cleaning out the dark, musty attic just before she moved out, too old to
  live there any more.

But not many words came out of that house.

In later years, my grandmother would sit in a high-backed chair in front of a
  window,
away from the bustle and noise of family, motionless except for her hands,
which danced and flitted above her lap like the wings of a humming bird.

Those hands were large and gnarled, like the bark of a tree.
Farmer's hands,
fingers long and callused from years of hard labor.
Yet when I touched those hands they felt cool and smooth and clear,
as if they were polished with a layer of shiny wax.

Things grew out of those hands sweaters for grandchildren,
quilted blankets for cold winter evenings, doilies as intricate as spider webs.
They spread into bedrooms and living rooms and kitchen tables all across the
    country
like coded messages, secret hieroglyphics,
their meaning deeply woven into the fabric of each object,
to be uncovered and read over and over again,
long after the farmer's hands quit moving.

Just Like New

Adam J. Johnson

Thirty years old,
it still works for rich gas and oil.
When it's working, it blows the bad air
out,
the black exhaust,
sailing behind me.
I lower the disk,
It breaks the soil and tears up the ground,
like a dog digging,
I slow her down to give her a break,
popping just like a new tractor.

Centreville Junior High School

The High Seat

Rose R. Burket

Now this is a story someone told my mother.

Once there was a minister coming to Millburg as a candidate for one of the churches. He was coming by train, and an Elder of the church went to meet him. The Elder had a lumber wagon, with a very high seat. Now in those days, Territorial was a very good road, it was a gravel road and well maintained. The other roads were dirt roads, so people would cross over to use Territorial Road whenever they could, but there was one place on Territorial, where it goes across the creek, I think by Park Street, you probably wouldn't notice it today, especially in a car, and they've leveled it off, but in those days, the road went down and up a steep hill. Farmers always got off their wagons and walked up the hill to make it easier for their horses, so when the Elder's wagon got to that section, he got down from his wagon before the horses pulled it up the hill. The minister did not get off, he sat on the high seat the whole time the horses were working hard to get the wagon up the hill, I think it was called Sutton Hill, I'm not sure. Well, the Elder was so angry at this man who would not get down and walk for the sake of the horses that he told everyone in the congregation, told how the man just sat there and let the horses pull him up that hill. The candidate did not get the job.

The Simpler Times

Logan Witt

Please stop and consider
And tell if you would,
Are the simpler times
Really gone for good?

A buck in those times
Were of silver and gold,
and you received full pay
For the things you sold.

You would shake a man's hand
And look him in the eye,
With this Agreement
You would sell and buy.

You'd welcome a stranger
And share a hot meal,
With very little thought
Of what he would steal.

Out in the country
In a one room school,
We learned the three R's
And the old golden rule.

We all said the pledge
And all bowed to pray,
No one told us,
"You can't do things that way."

A date with your girl
I'm sure you all know,
Was a fifty cent trip
To the neighborhood show.

Then for a sweet treat.
With never a flaw,
A twenty cent soda,
Two spoons and two straws.

Each family had a shed
With a moon on the door,
A mail order catalog
Laid on the floor.

A Ford and a Chevy
Ran ten years, as they should
with no strange noises
From under the hood.

Our cellars were all full,
But no one would brag.
We got Eight O'clock coffee
In a red paper bag.

We'd go to church on Sunday
With the Lord we would speak,
Then back for Prayer service
In the middle of the week.

I could go on, but,
The time I'll not take.
I think you get the point
I'm trying to make.

So stop and consider
And be honest as you should.
I feel the simpler times
Are really gone for good.

My Summer Friends

Judy G. McLain

Sometime after the orchards had all been covered with pink blossoms as far as I could see in almost any direction, I knew it was time for my Summer Friends to come!

If I did not see the caravan of cars driving up the hill when they arrived, I would awaken to very soft guitar music in the gentle darkness of night. My heart would jump and I strained to hear the soothing strumming—the time had come!

My Summer Friends lived in the back pasture the several weeks they were with us and while normally I had the run of the farm, I was not allowed to intrude on my friends' family time after the cherries were picked for the day.

My Summer Friends probably did not speak English and I spoke no Spanish but we had no difficulty understanding each other when we plunked down under the cherry tree nearest our parents, as they moved through the rows of trees. We would move our dolls and toys from tree to tree and watch the stack of filled cherry lugs get higher and higher as the day grew longer. The cherries glistened in the sunshine and we ate quite a lot of them so looking for other food would not interrupt our play.

My father could pick as many lugs of cherries in a day as any of my friends' parents could. That made me feel good.

It was a sad time when my Summer Friends had to move on to work at their next farm. Fruit farms take up lots of space so neighbors were too far away to visit. The summer grew long and lonely after my summer friends left.

The sadness I felt when the dusty cars drove back down the hill and out of sight was made only slightly less hurtful because I knew the pink blossoms would come again, summer would arrive, the cherries would get heavy on the trees and MY SUMMER FRIENDS WOULD COME BACK TO ME!

Packing Isn't the Hardest Part of Moving

Melissa Dine

I draped myself across the fuzzy tan chair
As we finished up another Friday movie night at Jake's
My comfortable pose froze
Like the pause button was on
Then in slow-motion
I heard Jake speak
"I'm moving when school gets out."
I was floating in some other world
Watching the tall, dark haired, cow lover
Mouth words I didn't want to hear
I wanted to turn off this movie
Best friends can't live on opposite sides of the country
How far is it from Michigan to Oregon?
I couldn't turn it off
"oh" is all I could speak out

The movie fast forwarded
My tan chair was moved
Boxes stood in its place
Cartons full of rooms
A whole family's life
stored in brown cardboard
Rooms waiting to expand back to their shapes
In another house
In another state
I just wanted my chair back
Thunder rolled

We went outside the split-level house
For the last time
We laughed and hugged
While jumping in the newly formed puddles
I wanted to rewind and
Replay the last 45 minutes of this movie

But I didn't have the remote control
So I let the rain hide my tears.

St. Joseph High School

In the Heat of the Summer

Marie E. Kelley

On Sunday morning, July 14, 1996, at 10:45 a.m., I approached the ten acre site that had been my home for the first ten years of my life. In fifteen minutes, the fire departments would arrive to burn the house to the ground. On July 5, as the auctioneer sang out his sales spiel and enticed the many strangers in the yard to buy tools and toys that rewove the fabric of my early life, I had walked around the house and noticed the storm windows behind the bushes on the north side of the house. I'd wanted to save something from the house, but not just anything. What I saved would have to be useful. I had been wanting to make a cold frame to extend my gardening season; I would use the storm windows for it. Dad would approve, if he were alive. I had just 15 minutes to load them into my minivan. As I was loading, I noticed that one of the four windows was longer than the others. I needed four windows the same size. I walked to the east side of the house and saw that one storm window was still attached to the window frame. The firemen were arriving in their engines and tanker trucks, so I asked one of them to remove the window. When it was loaded, I moved my minivan down the road, away from the house.

Then, I took my video camera and began to shoot and talk as I walked through the yard that held so many memories. I focused on the big maple tree in the front yard. Dad had attached the ropes of our swing to one of its branches. The branch was high and the ropes long so we could swing high into the air. One year, when I was older, Baltimore Orioles built a nest in its high branches. The front yard was the site of many pictures in the family album, one with my father carrying me in a bushel basket on his shoulder, another of a three year old me giving my rubber doll a bath in an enameled basin, just the way Mom bathed us kids in the tiny kitchen of the house with no bathroom. The front yard was where I posed for a picture with my grandfather Foerch before going off to the Little Brick School for my first day of kindergarten. That school had been torn down many years ago, and the school in town where I had attended grades four through 12 and began my teaching career had been leveled last year. How ironic, when the school that my grandmother Foerch had attended was still standing. Now, I was about to witness the deliberate destruction of the home of my birth.

My father, who died last May at the age of 88 years and eight months, was a "do-it-yourself" man, stingy with the fortune he and my mother had made on the evergreen nursery that once embellished this small ten acre plot of sandy ground. The summer before he turned 87, he climbed up on the roof with tar to patch the roof. But his patch didn't last, and the raccoons ransacked the attic, going in and out through the holes in the roof. The rain came in and soaked through the ceilings. Dad had put plastic over the ancient furniture and the floors, but the plastic only served to catch the rain and create pools of water. On July 5, I'd gone up in the attic with my brother to check out the auctioneer's rejects. The attic stairway came down into our bedroom. I remembered how, as a very little girl, I'd have nightmares about Baba Yaga, a supposedly friendly witch who was a frequent character of stories in the *Jack and Jill* magazine, coming down those stairs to take me away. That little bedroom had housed four children. My sister and I had separate double beds, and my brothers' cribs lined the east wall. Crayon marks decorated that wall. (My brothers were four and two when we moved to town.)

I continued my journey through the yard. The wild daylilies under the trees in the south lawn had survived the many years of my playmates and me carving out "rooms" by stomping them down. The lilies of the valley were even more profuse than they'd been when I was a kid. The boxwood was gone, though. One Christmas during my crafty preteen years, I'd harvested boughs of boxwood to make a dark green ball of foliage to surround a swig of mistletoe. An old plastic bucket covered the pump where I'd pumped water for the laundry and for washing the produce Dad took to Lansing market before the nursery business days. I remember when Dad piped cold water to the kitchen sink. We had an icebox in the basement before we bought our first refrigerator that worked until we gave it away on July 5. Once, I went into the damp basement barefooted. I reached up to pull the chain on the light; a shock ran from my fingertip to my toes and out into the dirt floor. When I was older, I was taunting my brother, six years my junior, by waving the cellar door up and down as he stood on the steps below it. The door slipped, hit him and raised a big goose egg on his head. Was I penitent! On July 5, he'd struggled to remove the pulley that held the weight to that door so his wife could use it as a hanger for plants on her porch.

I walked past the site of the dinner bell standard. From the time I was ten until I went away to college, I cooked lunch for the family and the hired boys. When the food was ready, I'd ring the dinner bell, and its pleasant tones would vibrate through the air, calling everyone to a meal and midday rest. Ahead of me was the garage. It was one of my favorite places. Our mother cat would usually hide her kittens behind the boxes of sample copies of magazines Dad sold for Curtis Publishing Company. A big, pot bellied stove stood in the corner of the garage. One day when I was seven, Mom took my brother off to the doctor, and I decided to play in the garage. I found some candles and matches and ignited the papers in the stove. After all, it was a stove, why not let it serve its purpose? I didn't realize that the stove needed to be hooked up to a chimney to work safely. Dad came to the rescue and put out that fire. I begged him not to tell Mom about it. He agreed. One day when I was about 12 years old, Mom made reference to that fire. I felt as though Dad had betrayed me. When I was older, I understood the need for parents to communicate about the activities of their children, and forgave Dad for breaking that promise.

Beyond the garage was the outhouse. It was my job to empty the chamber pots we used in the house at night. Now, deep green and prolific, the myrtle covered the ground near the outhouse, choking out the rhubarb that used to flourish there. Further west were the tool sheds. Dad had fixed a shelf for the radio in the 1950's so we could listen to the MSU football games as we waited on customers in the fall. Making a circle toward the north side of the house, I surveyed the Schwederle maple tree Grandpa Foerch had planted in 1940. Now, it was the parent of a forest of Norway maple trees that surrounded it.

Back in the front yard, I heard the clamor of shattering glass as a fireman struck the windows with a metal-tipped pole. Another man took a flaming torch into the house. Red orange flames surged through the front door. Then, more flames leaped through the windows. Minutes later, they devoured the roof, and the side walls began to crumble inward. This was Dad's funeral pyre. The firemen sprayed the trees with water, a feeble gesture to protect them from the flames. My video camera battery was dead. I put it in the car and picked black raspberries as I watched the smoldering fire, filling my water bottle with plump, purple gems.

The next morning, I returned to the scene with a freshly charged battery to capture the scene up close. Little wisps of smoke curled upward from the foundation of that tiny house that held so many memories. The basement cavity enclosed pieces of chimney, bed springs, the kitchen range and other debris. Soon, some men Mom had hired would fill the hole with gravel, burying the artifacts of my childhood.

Home

Mary G. DeYoung

I visit my childhood home
and find it in ruins
reinvented as a forest.
The house once stood here
where ash trees now stand.
The barn, there
a rise in the ground where it was.
Fenceposts mark boundaries,
holding remnants of wire—
keeping out or
keeping in?
the emptiness
rustles with dry leaves
and broken branches.

My memories race.
Here I stood when
I held the reins of the horse
that was gentle enough for me
to ride alone.
There I played with the black and white dog.
I watched the horses graze in that pasture
every day of my childhood.
I remember kicking the soccer ball
against the barn wall
for hours.

I can see the place where my sister
planted a garden
according to her plan on paper.
Sometimes we read under the big maple
exploring a world we couldn't know.
I imagine the place where she stood
joyful next to her husband of an hour.

I can imagine my father's stocky shape
moving around the out buildings
tending to endless tasks.
On the mowing machine
preferring the roan team to tractor,
he slowly harvested the hay.
Often he would stop his work
to take out the trained pony
or tease us until we cried.

I can see my mother worrying her way
through the daily tasks of a farm wife,
always consumed by the duties of her role.
Shelling peas, baking bread,
canning the hard little pears
because they grew there,
she filled her day
with work—
never too busy to read to us
every afternoon before dinner.

Engorged with memory,
I retrace my steps from
my childhood home.

It's what I call my "Earth Mother" phase

Pamela M. Buchanan

In the early 70's we were young, idealistic and poor.
Well, we didn't know it or see it that way—
after all we had a house, a car, jobs/school,
and space to move around.
We shared ten acres with my in-laws,
but were separated by nearly a city block,
and surrounded by farm fields and wooded land.
We thought we had it all.

Our first garden was over an acre.
We planted everything from peas and potatoes to cabbage and kohlrabi,
enough to feed the proverbial army
(Or at least most of our family and friends!)
I learned to weed, pick, shell, husk, blanch, freeze, jell,
even how to pressure can like my Gram had done.

We bought flour and sugar in 25 pound bags, and
yeast and spices in bulk from the local food co-op.
I baked all of our bread, cookies, pies, and cakes from scratch.
Aromas of yeast and sourdough, rye with caraway, whole grain
with sorghum, chocolate and cinnamon filled the air.
The kitchen became the hub—the center of the house
and family.

We fed our family and friends—rarely did we have a weekend
meal where the table was set only for three.
Family, sure, but more often friends from the city ventured out,
escaping small apartments for the house on the hill.
They'd bring the wine or the ice cream—
or the fixings to fill the old hand crank ice cream maker,
rescued from the attic at my in-laws.
They'd work in the garden or help in the preparation
and take home what was excess to us, but riches to them.

The satisfaction that came from providing for others
only added to our already rich lives.
We really did have it all.

Making rhubarb pie with a thirteen-year-old

Pen Campbell

Well, first stand up.
You can't roll out a pie crust sitting down.
Now put some flour on the pastry sheet.
Not that much—just
a little.
You're sprinkling it. You want
your hand to sweep above the cloth,
broadcast a dust of flour fine as talcum
evenly.
Turn your hand over. Here
Like this . . .
and sweeeeeeeeep
like feeding chickens.
Too much flour ruins pie crust.
Okay, now some on top.
Okay.
Now take the rolling pin and don't
press down. See . . .
Roll and
turn the pin
Roll and
turn the pin
And now the crust
Just slip your hands beneath the crust like this
Gently
and turn the whole thing.
Here.
Now roll . . . just up to the edge . . .
Just right. up. to. the edge.
Not over.
That's why it's sticking.
It will get bigger . . . rounder . . . evenly
you don't need to go over the edge.
Gently

Roll
and turn the pin
Gently.
Roll
and turn the pin
You don't want to work it too much.
Just a light touch
Gently.
Everything with pie crust should be gentle.

My Mom

Cheryl Sears

My mom's eyes shine
Like the North Star.
Her hair shines like the
Ocean's surface. Her yells are
Like a steaming kettle.

She stands over
The hot oven
Everyday cooking
Supper after 10 hours
of working in Indiana,
at Robert Plywood Inc.

She teaches me
What it means
To be a mom.

Centreville Junior High School

A Winter of Sorrow

Brittany Lynn Doyle

I walked out into the garage. A sudden chill ran through my body, freezing my veins. I saw my breath, I walked on.

I felt cold but despite the bitterness of that Michigan winter I felt joyful. A few days prior, my gray cat had brought three kittens in to this world owned by Jack Frost.

Better yet, they were calico! My favorite type of cat ever since Molly Moon. Molly Moon is my cat, or used to be. Her coat was part calico part white. No special cat in breed but in my heart she was the grand champion of every cat there ever was or ever will be. But in this world I live next to a street. The street has cars zooming by . . . fast, with no time to stop. Molly Moon simply stepped in front of one of those zooming cars and was gone in the blink of an eye.

But now I had a new place for my heart, the kittens. They seemed so fuzzy and little. You could hear their soft cries for milk. But they wanted something more. They wanted the warmth of a tropical island. Where mangos and pineapples grow. Where everyday the sun shines its warm rays upon the sand, removing all the chills from your body. No one could give them that but soon I sprang up on a new idea. I ran to the heat of the house to get a soft blanket.

I was stopped by the towering height of my mother. She knew my plans. She made it quite clear that the kittens needed to survive on their own and not with my help. I was resentful that I had run into my mother, but being the good little girl I was, I obeyed her.

The day passed, night came. I looked at the kittens once more and walked off to crawl in *my* bundle of blankets. That was the last time I would see the kittens breathing.

I awoke only to find three frozen bodies. I cried but I know that they must have a happy life in heaven. And someday, hopefully not too soon would reunite with their mother.

The cross upon their grave still stands though the strings tying the two sticks together is weak from facing the brutal seasons of my life. At four years old I had lost many pets but this story was one I was sure to remember.

Gull Lake Middle School

Gardening Lessons

Coral J. Fry

I loved visiting Grandmother in the summer.
She would garden in the sun
bent at the waist
curved like one of the horseshoes
nailed to her draft horses' hooves.
She would clear a row of weeds,
say Look, see my good work done.

(What would she think of me?
Does a page full of writing help to put the world in order?
What about my weedy garden? Even here, it calls to me).

I would play in the soil,
mimic her actions,
amazed at the weeds
sprung up since last week
in my little earthenware pots.
I asked, Why do you have to plant the food
when the weeds grow by themselves?
The weeds are planted by the wind, she said.

The Herb Cottage

Ashley B. Mikulyuk

For as long as I can remember, my grandma has come to our house every Saturday morning. She would always bring donuts and fruit and other little treats for my sister and I. My favorite were the jelly-filled donuts. I remember just eating the jelly then throwing the dough part away!!

My grandma, who I call Bema, used to come Thursdays, Fridays and Saturdays. This is because she used to run a tiny store called "The Herb Cottage."

The Herb Cottage was very homey. There were two rooms, one that we added on after we moved into our house.

The bigger room had rusty red roosters stenciled on the walls which were an off-white color. There were garlands of dried herbs hanging lifelessly on old splintery beams in the ceiling.

Most of the furniture we had in the Herb Cottage was given to us by friends, or we bought them at an auction. All of them were antiques and very grand-looking. Such as a towering cupboard that we put bags of seasoning and soup mix in. It reminded me of an old, tattered war veteran that was very proud. There was a large, red brick fireplace that had a wooden beam over the top of it. We hung dried herbs, copper pots, hand-dipped candles and many different seasonal decorations. The fireplace added to the log cabin look of the Herb Cottage.

This shop was one of my favorite places. Everywhere you looked there was something new. My grandma loved to look for things she wanted to sell, many of which would never sell!

She always had things for me to do. My favorite thing to do was to play with the cash register. Sometimes I'd get to serve a customer. I remember one time I was ringing up a customer and when I was done the total was over ten thousand dollars! I had to do the whole thing over again.

One of the neatest things in the shop was an old, black wood stove that was made out of a barrel. It had a small, circle, latched door where you could throw firewood into. On top of the barrel, my grandma would melt scented wax to create a calming aroma of cinnamon. The stove would make the room feel just like home. When the winter days got too cold, we had to switch on the furnace. We still kept the fire lit because it smelled so nicely.

During store hours, my grandma would help the customers, plant things in our garden, and do an enormous amount of things like that. My mother would make the prettiest dried flower arrangements. She used so many different flowers, and they all came from the garden. There were bunches of sweet-smelling baby's breath, every kind of herb you could imagine, and my favorite was the lavender. It was so tiny and so fragrant. Although the flowers were all dried up, they had the neatest colors. There were light mauve, dark forest green, rosy red, canary yellow, and every color that anyone could imagine! When you put all of the arrangements together it looked like a rainbow made of flowers and herbs.

When my mom went back to work, it was just the two of us, Bema and I. Occasionally we did have a few employees, but they just ended up getting fired or quitting. I guess you could say they didn't fit in with our routine!

The Herb Cottage was in business for quite a while. But it got to the time when my grandma couldn't keep up with it anymore. She loves to travel, and is always busy. One lady we talked to wanted to buy the Herb Cottage, but my grandma, my mom and my dad never made it final. I think they didn't want anyone else to have it either!

Edwardsburg Middle School

Going to My Aunt's House

Amy Prater

I love to go to my aunt's house. Her name is Amy. She has a little baby. His name is Jeffrey, Jr. He is 9 months old. They have lived there a long time. She lives in a green trailer. She has a husband named Jeff. Her trailer is so much fun!

Most times I go there, Aunt Amy and I make chocolate-chip cookies. Or, I take the baby in the stroller on a walk down to get the mail. We stay and wait until Aunt Amy comes back. After we get back from the mail, the baby takes a nap. We go and do the laundry and move the furniture around. Then we eat lunch. We eat tacos. She has four dogs now, but she used to have ten dogs and a cat. Me and her and her baby do a lot of stuff together. I spend the night with her a lot.

Colon Elementary School

Small Town Life

Erica L. Stewart

Richland is a sleepy small town in Southern Michigan. I've lived here all my life. The people of our town have always kept it from modernizing too much. Fast food chains have been prohibited and now the only restaurant is a small town pizzeria called Sajo's next to the Richland Bowling Alley. When I was younger my brother would pick me up from school and we'd go there to eat the great tasting pizza. As a child the walk seemed like miles but it's really only a few blocks. Sometimes we'd see the town hobo that roams the streets of Richland in search of a ride or some money. He carries all his possessions in an orange back pack. Sometimes you can hear him singing as you pass him.

The old school buildings and town hall stand as reminders of another time. The trees in the central park have been there forever. The one school building seems like an intruder in a memory with its glass roofs and big modern classrooms.

The only traffic light in town is never too busy except during Homecoming or when the whole town turns out to go singing door to door at Christmas. I've done that many times and I love the hot cocoa they serve afterwards at the town hall. The big red library has many old and new books. It has a very creaky floor and it smells like the bindings of the oldest books. Next to it, the old white-washed Presbyterian Church stands tall. It owns the playground that the preschool uses for its students. Some of my earliest memories are of playing on the sea-saw during recess at preschool.

In conclusion I think life in my small-town is just perfect.

Gull Lake Middle School

Richland, a Small Boring Town

Adam Burghdoff

Richland is old fashioned.
It moves too slow
But just right for people eighty and older.
The town grocery store
Is but a speck
Compared to Meijer's.
The formal restaurant
Is an old hotel
Converted
To a restaurant
Nobody eats there
Except for the Lion's Club
On Tuesday afternoons at 12:00.
The old town has more banks than people.
Overall Richland is considered old fashioned.

Gull Lake Middle School

Langley Covered Bridge: A Michigan Milestone

Douglas Andrew Schrock

At sunset, the mist of the long, winding, and beautiful St. Joseph River enshrouds the Covered Bridge. Filtered rays of sunlight, mixed in with clouds of blue, purple, orange, violet, and bright, fiery red, pour down upon it, lighting up its sides like a flame. A monument of red, it stands out as one of the most important pieces of St. Joseph County history. Despite these wonderful depictions of our county's most famous and most widely visited landmark, it is forgotten by those who live within a mile of it. However, I have tried to urge myself to remember it, to acknowledge its presence, its history, and its beauty.

Langley Covered Bridge, named for Centreville's famous pioneer family, was built in 1887 by Pierce Bodner, a construction tycoon in then-booming Parkville, a town that would, in the early 1900s, become a community with a thinned-out population and only a mark on well-detailed state maps. Two hundred eighty-two feet long, Langley would become the only covered bridge in St. Joseph County and the longest in all of Michigan, an honor it still boasts to this day.

In 1910, the Sturgis Power Company built a dam within view of the bridge. The bridge was raised eight feet, in order to preserve this legacy of our county's rich, yet forgotten, history: great Indian battles, pioneer villages, old trails crucial to passengers between Detroit and Chicago, land offices, and many other important sites and Southwestern Michigan's relics of the past.

Forty years later, in 1950, extensive repairs were done to the siding and 54-foot spans of the bridge. Due to this work, finished in 1951, it looks quite new and well-preserved to this day. In 1965, a historical marker was erected to point out to both tourists and locals alike the Covered Bridge's important place in St. Joseph County.

Although much of the Covered Bridge topic deals with facts and data, it is important to the heart, not just the brain. It is very sentimental to me. In my first days of living in Michigan, trying to make the transition from living in Richmond, Virginia my whole life, I rarely even looked at the bridge. Instead, I took it for granted and did not let its bright red paint and more than 250 feet of wood sink in. I failed to look at it in a way that would say, "I appreciate this bridge and hope it lasts for as long as I do, if not longer."

I now cringe when someone makes a sarcastic or mocking reply to a positive comment about the bridge, such as, "Who cares? It's been there for years," or "It's just an inconvenience when you're in a rush." People don't realize until it is too late that these sorts of negative remarks can lead to complete shunning of important historical sites, such as the Covered Bridge or the White Pigeon land office, and, if a serious enough case, destruction of these places. It is our duty to preserve these places, and pass their legacies on to future generations. I always get a feeling of happiness and relief when I see a family riding their bikes and reading the marker or staring at the bridge in wonderment from Pahl Point.

I am awed whenever I cross the bridge's worn wooden planks, whether on foot, in an automobile, or on a bicycle. At Covered Bridge County Park, just down the road, I will stand on top of the dike, and look half-a-mile across the still waters and just stare at it for a time. A great blue heron swoops over my head, a killdeer cries out in the distance, a raccoon scuttles subtly through the brush, looking for berries or a small animal to snack on. Pahl Point looms out into the river, its dock a dark square of wood encircling a swamp of reeds and bulrushes. The sun sinks, swallowed up by the horizon masked by the woods behind me.

I travel through the park's looping trails, my legs brush against the rich green ferns, I duck beneath dead branches, watch bugs skitter across the pond water, hear the running water in the drain, swat at mosquitoes on my legs, rays of fading sunlight trying sneakily to just faintly slip through the trees, and getting a grasp on my neck.

A squirrel chirps, gathers an acorn or two, and runs back across the path in front of me. A bright red male cardinal tweets and flies above me, chased by another for the love of a mate. Feisty robins challenge each other for food and territory. Life goes on. Nature runs its course.

Then I come through to the clearing, and there it is, through the trees and across the river. There it always will be, and has been, since and before I first journeyed to this domain. As long as I am here, I hope to always see it there, looming nearly three hundred feet across the water, rising above carp and bass, in a world of nature and nostalgia . . . the Covered Bridge.

Centreville Junior High School

Fishing Off the Pier

E. Kevin Owens

If you came to St. Joseph and you were a fisherman, you would want to go fishing off the pier. We have two piers. I recommend fishing off the pier with the lighthouse on it. This is a pier swarming with fish.

One of the biggest and most rarely caught fish is the Michigan White Fish. I have caught only one and *Michigan Outdoors*, a TV show, had me on it for catching it. It is a big fish and in my opinion delicious.

The Coho is a big fish that is caught all the time. It tastes good smoked. It is brown with dots on its belly. They put up a good fight. The Rainbow Trout is usually a 7"-9" fish, and fat. It is a silver fish with pretty colored dots on its belly. It is a good tasting fish too.

If you like to fish and like to catch fish you know where to come. St. Joseph is a great fishing hole. Now I hope you come to St. Joseph to go fishing.

Lincoln Elementary School

Noon Whistle

Tom Anderson

The railroad tracks and country highways
dissect our town like love and money.
Trains come at irregular times and
irregular speeds but never stop.
Semis roll through the midsection,
but people have learned not to notice.
Retired teachers live across from school.
The old pastor, his wife,
and familiar names
are buried in the cemetery
next to church.
In the restaurant
men sit and smoke,
and never have to order.
They drive slow in big cars,
and relish Sundays with their grandchildren.
Even the ice melts slowly
in Grandma's flat Coke.
People take deep breaths;
cry only at funerals.
Across the tracks things keep pace.
Tucked along the highway
pizza places and ice cream stands
have grand openings
and quiet closings.
Girls slurp rootbeer floats
after softball, win or lose.
Truckers refuel
where cheerleaders and ball players
go for pre-game
Mountain Dew and candy.
No one still farms, but
vinyl homes fringe a landscape

of corn and soybean.
Here people swear as the train stops traffic and
the noon whistle goes unheard.

Jovon

Pen Campbell

I caught a Skamania once
Almost.
One morning in July
for maybe two, three minutes
I had one.
After walking down the gray dawn pier
and easing quietly, humbly, into place
standing shoulder to shoulder with the men.
After carefully not hearing
their man whispers
voices barely softened
That a woman down there
next to Jack?
Can't tell. 's got a hat on.
About eleven, I got one.
I was casting
the expected Little Cleo
with a stripe of teal
the men called green.
It hit like a rocket.
Like Moby Dick
on Angel Dust
it ran

bam jump
bam jump
fast angry graceful gone
I clenched till twelve
so they wouldn't see my hands shake.

I thought of that Skamania
Jovon
the day we added fractions.
As I trolled ideas

through deep impenetrable blue
and felt the hit
bam answer
bam walk right up to the board
right in my face to answer
bam bam
fastangrygracefulgone
I clenched till twelve
so they wouldn't see my hands shake.

Monte

Tom Anderson

Monte Johnson was the best farm hand I have ever seen. In 1985 he was also the biggest, meanest, and most talented football player at our school. Farmers loved him; he worked fast and hard, refusing to take a break until the last mound was filled and wagon unloaded.

When they called him to work, the farmers always asked him to bring a friend. Probably because I was the only person who would put up with his abuse, Monte chose me as his partner. We were a team, and a good one. At times we were in such demand, we had to turn work down.

Since I was only 15, Monte would pick me up in the morning. His rusted, red pickup with the shift on the column had the familiar smell of old motor oil, alfalfa, and sun baked vinyl. We had to be careful not to push our feet through the floorboards when we got in, and when there were puddles in the road, the water splashed into the cab. The tailgate was held together with baling twine. Beneath the driver's seat Monte had two prized possessions, his tin of Kodiak, which made me sick, and his dirty magazines which I didn't mind so much. Monte raced that thing like a mad man. I was terrified, but loved every minute of it.

The Paulens were among our favorite farmers to work for. They paid relatively well and usually ordered pizza for us at the end of the day. Monte and I were in charge of unloading the wagon and filling the mound; sometimes we had someone else to help us but not often. As usual Monte would take charge. He sent me into the mound to stack the bales, while he stood below, furiously trying to unload the first wagon before the next would arrive. It was a matter of pride to him to know that he could unload the hay faster than they could bale it. He would file the bales on the elevator end to end and sometimes even on top of each other up to the mound where I was helplessly being buried in alfalfa or clover. Inevitably I would have to beg him to slow down or stop. After piling on a few more bales Monte would shut off the machine and shout angrily, "What the hell are you doing up there?"

I would always have to admit that I couldn't keep up. Scrambling into the mound, Monte would mutter angrily, "Jesus Christ. . . . You're always cobbling it up." And then he'd continue with a smile "and you call me to decobble your mess." I'm certain that he took pride during these moments of superiority. He was the one who fixed things, made them right. I hated admitting at the time, he was the best. Monte turned my haphazard chaos into neatly filled mounds; absent of wasted space.

What taking my son to the army taught me about claustrophobia

Dan Holt

It was early,
4 a.m.,
when we started for Lansing
on a journey to the meps station,
the dropping off point,
the place where fathers
take their sons to become soldiers.
Quietly slipping
through the Michigan countryside,
we talked
about a possible steelhead run,
the pennant race,
the oil leak,
about everything but his leaving.

The way we pushed
that away
reminded me of
when I was a kid
and my father
brought home a whirl-e-gig
that made my sister and me
sick from the circles
we did in the backyard.

And so,
dizzy from our circular
conversation, I let him go.
He pulled his suitcase
from the back of the truck
and walked away,
looking back only once,
but I couldn't

make out his face
with the sun
rising over
his shoulder that way.

As I drove home,
the cab felt too small
now that he was gone,
no air left to breathe.
A buzzing in my ears.
I pulled over,
stumbled from the truck,
sick to my stomach,
but too empty to vomit.

A Father's Expression of Love

Renee Callies

With his eighteen-month-old daughter leading him by the hand, my brother Todd squawked and quacked, oblivious to the silliness of his antics, in a futile attempt to convince the geese and ducks at the bird sanctuary to imitate his babble. Shoving aside the video camera draped over his shoulder, he bent down to peer in his daughter's face. "Isabel! Look at all the duckies! What do duckies say . . . huh?! Quwack . . . quwack . . . quwack. Can you say that?"

"Cawk, cawk, cawk," Isabel mimicked Todd dutifully, then stuck her hand out and stepped towards the geese, hoping they would come take the corn clenched in her fist. I realized that at the same time my brother unself-consciously entertained the gathered audience, he taught his daughter, in an easy give-and-take dialogue, the sounds that identified the animals. As we followed behind, my friend, a father himself, expressed envy for the relationship he saw fathers and children having today. Both he and my own father grew up and raised families at a time when nurturing remained strictly a maternal concept.

I'm not sure when Todd learned to rock a cranky infant to sleep, or count toes in childish dialect. Certainly with the increase in single-parent families and joint-custody, he has witnessed, firsthand, the ways parenting roles have changed and expanded. Women, typically the "nurturers," have increasingly assumed financial responsibility for the house. Likewise, in an effort to connect with their children, more men play games, ask questions, share stories and devote time with families.

My father missed these opportunities of spontaneity my brother enjoys. I grew up in a traditional family: Mom stayed at home and assumed all the roles of nurturer, healer and general disciplinarian, while Dad left the house and earned a living. Preoccupied with keeping his electrical contracting business afloat, he had time for few distractions, including his children. Because of this, I felt he ignored my developmental needs, which, along with normal hormonal angst, put a strain on our relationship during my teenage years. Unless he checked on grades, divvied up chores, or ruled on disputes, our conversations were minimal. Unfortunately, the dinner table, the only place we gathered as a family each day, became the spot to air grievances and irritations.

I can remember several meals when lectures served as punishment for our misdeeds. Trying to eat while holding back tears made it impossible to swallow, and that lump in my throat would grow with Dad's disappointment. The demise of our pet rabbit was preceded by one such conversation. My father, sitting at the head of the table, filled his plate and began.

"Who was supposed to clean the rabbit's cage?" Caught unawares, none of us—neither my sister, my brother nor I—said anything, instead focusing on the mashed potatoes, the green beans, the meat loaf covering our plates. "Why does your mother have to feed it?" Again, no one spoke, hoping the other would find the courage to offer an explanation. "What's the sense of keeping an animal if you're not going to take care of it?" his voice stayed calm, but firm. Cornered, we knew we had to try and convince Dad that our inaction was justified.

"We didn't do it on purpose; we just forgot," my sister, picking at her potatoes, explained.

"We'll take care of Fluffy from now on, we promise," I added, tears starting to well in my eyes. It was true; we hadn't cleaned the cage, hadn't fed the rabbit. We were at fault, irresponsible, and we knew it. Pleading wouldn't sway Dad.

"No. I've given you too many chances already. I'll take care of it." And he did. The cage stood empty for several years after that, until we finally broke it apart and discarded it.

Today, as I listen to Todd and Isabel's carefree conversations, I realize that although the communication between my father and me was often forced and sometimes unhappy, it never meant a lack of love. I remember when my dad constructed a basketball hoop for me; the solemnity of the event, the desire for my input, the emphasis on my help and his gentle guidance served as unspoken expressions of affection.

I started playing basketball in seventh grade and used our old backboard attached to the garage to practice. I showed enthusiasm for the sport and tenacity for practice, so after I started playing for the high school team, Dad decided it was time I had an "official" hoop to use. Securing my interest, Dad told me prior to putting up the board that I would need to look up the correct dimensions and height of the pole and board; meanwhile, he would scavenge for a large aluminum pole from work and purchase a piece of plywood from the lumberyard.

On a summer weekend, using the dimensions I found in our *World Book Encyclopedia*, we carefully measured, then drew the backboard shape on the plywood. While I watched, he cut it out with a table saw, and together, we painted it white. After attaching the board to the pole, we dug a three-foot hole, poured concrete into the depression, and with my brother's help, placed the pole carefully into the opening, making sure it was plumb with a level. After we repainted the old hoop bright orange, we attached it to the backboard, measuring from the ground to the basket to verify the rim stood at ten feet. With the concrete still wet, Dad insisted I make an imprint of my initials and the date, August, 1975.

This exposure to the camaraderie of craftsmanship was one of my first. In later years, this man would show me how to prune raspberry bushes, score a game of horseshoes, change a flat tire, and, across telephone lines, install a dimmer switch. With the sale of his business and with age, my father has mellowed, and our conversations have naturally relaxed. Like an animal freed after years of captivity, he follows his instincts. Now, he laughs a little more, says "I love you" a little more, and anticipates building another basketball hoop—for his granddaughter.

"TEAM!"

Lilly Massa

Leaving the huddle, where anything is possible
Stepping onto the court, where we have to prove it
The ladies are long gone
Sweated camouflage, bruised disguise
"Red on a make, blue on a miss"
echoes in my ear
Coveting that fragile egg
matching out heartbeats.
Step in time
Steal
Sting of attitude on my face.
"Fist, tell everyone . . . Fist!"
    Sting of stupor on my face
    Right block, here I come
My stomach tightens
my hands clench
Please, please, please
is the only prayer I can manage . . .
shoot!
I see Blood in the back of my head
taking off his glasses
wondering if they really work.
Whistle blowing brings me back to reality.
Exhausted, I take my seat on the bench
wishing my name wasn't Lilly.

St. Joseph High School

Visiting Hour

Mary Ann Wehler

*If this were played upon a stage now, I could
condemn it as improbable fiction.*

—*Shakespeare*

I ring the locked ward buzzer, think, *How did you hang
yourself, with all these precautions? Oh Anne, Oh Anne.*
The guard visually checks me through a window, lets
me in, points over to the "activity room." Past the pool
table, the bandaged cue sticks, the ping pong table,
the coffee machine, you sit in a long sleeved sweat
shirt. It hides scars you tore in your arms. Rope burns
circle your neck. A man sits and weeps. An anorexic
woman fills her coffee cup, clutches a smashed cigarette
wanders in and out. A teenage boy, four inch vertical
scars across arteries on his neck, comes in, cases the area,
leaves. I visit you. My heart pounds, I want to hold you,
rock you, I remind myself not to cry. You can't leave
this room, can't even sit on the patio. You hurt yourself.
A staff person shadows you, sits, looks at a magazine,
glances at us over the top, takes notes on a clipboard,
listens to our small talk. Stiff from Thorazine, a woman
in a housecoat walks in like a robot. Every patient
holds a cigarette. Smoking's allowed for ten minutes,
at ten minutes to the hour. It's 7:48. A woman , about
seventy, sits across from us. *Two cigarettes an hour,
fourteen hours a day, three days, this is not enough!*
She is trying to decide if forty cigarettes, will last till
her son's next visit. You hung from your clothes in this
hospital unsupervised for two minutes. I am terrified.
You're not getting better, no place in Michigan can help.
A Denver clinic will take you at $20,000 a week. I have
the plane tickets. What else can I do? I feel so helpless.

The man weeps, the woman with stringy hair returns
for coffee; you wear a sweatshirt to cover your scars.
The temperature is 95 degrees. Visiting hour is over;
I kiss you good-bye, hug you and hug you. I choke and say,
Remember, I love you, Anne.
You reply, *I'm fighting to stay alive.*
On the way home, I stop at your sister's. The minute I get
in the house, my two grandchildren pull me up the stairs.
Come see my bedroom. Dean, three, puts his hands on his
hips, tilts his head with a look of *Well what do you think?*
I've seen the dump trucks, fire trucks, tow trucks,
all over the walls and sheets. Leah shouts, *My room, my
room!* They tear down the hall, climb into her crib. *Cover me,
cover me! Kiss me, kiss me!* I kiss them. *Say it. Say it!*
I say, *Don't let the bed bugs bite.* I close the door, they
jump up screaming. I open the door, they flop back down.
Cover me, cover me! Kiss me, kiss me. I see your eyes,
your curls, your fingers. I hear your voice.

My Mother's Cups

Janet Tower

My mother's cups still sit smartly in the glass-doored cupboard.
She delighted in having at her table
    This one: a wedding morning present from her mother.
    This one: from Helen, who shared her childhood and became her sister-
        friend.
    This one: from her daughter, bought on a nurse's vacation in Montana.
    This one: from Aunt Louise whose name is granite under the maple tree
        in the cemetery by the railroad tracks.

My mother, some of my mother, is there too.

Her last days she stared through the glass with dizzy dismay.
Her eyes darted and darkened, searching for the
Comfortable ordinariness of her life.

She struggled mightily, unmoving on the bed.
"Where did this one come from?"
"I know this one."
"I . . . know . . . this . . . one."

In the end we had to tape newspaper over the glass,
As if she knew this veil was one step in letting go.

Grandma's

Jenifer McCauslin

Grandma's
Warm, neat
Cooking, cleaning, sweeping
People, loving, caring, hugging
Fishing, hunting, mushrooming
Nice, messy
Grandpa's

Eagle Lake Elementary

Election Day

Patricia Grover Heyn

The importance of election day starts out in a mist, somewhere after I went back to Baroda to live with Grandma and Grandpa in the new—far older, smaller, and shabbier—house than they had when I left. When I lived with Grandma and Grandpa before I went to Aunt Bea's for those two years, "we" were still in the "big house," and it was. Large bedrooms upstairs, and on the first floor a very large kitchen, formal dining room, a sitting room which was the main gathering place, and in front of those, a pair of living rooms where my father's funeral had been. From the back hall, there had been the two offices designed for a physician, used by my father in his brief practice.

Now Grandma and Grandpa were in this small shabby house where I remembered the lady we called "Aunt Mary" had lived before I went away. She was gone now, and Grandpa had rented it when the bank took the big house, not even consulting Grandma about her different dwelling. Only the living room furniture, the wonderful, slick brown leather davenport and the two large chairs which Grandpa would still be using at the end of his life, was the same. There was no sign of household help, and Grandma and Grandpa talked about money.

For some reason I did not understand, Grandpa no longer had funerals in Baroda, although he put on his best light brown suit and dark green tie to help Uncle Mike with the funerals that he conducted. The big store down town was now empty except for some left-over arm chairs and folding chairs, and behind the partition half-way back in the store, some dusty caskets. Nobody ever talked about what had happened to the business. That's the way my family was. But Grandpa, who had always been health officer, was becoming more involved with village government.

Now I became aware of election days, but they had to take their turn. First came caucuses, I think, and then primaries, and then elections. Now that Grandpa was no longer in the undertaking business, he would rely on his township or village office to help pay our bills. And until he was eighty-seven, he would work being one or another of the squares on the ballot. Justice of the Peace, or treasurer or supervisor, Grandpa stayed busy. When he was health officer, he paid me a nickel for each SCARLET FEVER or SMALL POX or DIPTHERIA sign he needed, and I printed them on red cardboard, a slow job with a carpenter's pencil.

There was no township or village hall, not until years later, so elections were held in a variety of places. Once in the fire station, I think, cold and damp. And I think I remember one in the Ford auto showroom, but my favorite place was Grandpa's store.

Of course, it was used all spring and summer after Grandpa started selling fruit packages--strawberry and raspberry crates, bushel baskets, half-bushels, and containers for peaches, plums, pears, and tomatoes. And of course for all the other wonderful things farmers grew in that remarkably fertile, hospitable crescent along the edge of Lake Michigan. And in quiet times, Grandpa nailed together strawberry carriers, hoping farmers would buy them instead of making their own.

The first election I remember was the contest of Hoover against Roosevelt. Judging from the sentiment in our county newspaper, I was wondering why Roosevelt even bothered. The election became a topic of conversation everywhere I wandered, even among women. Grandma and Grandpa were for Roosevelt, but almost everyone else seemed to be for Hoover. Full of enthusiasm for this phenomenon in my life, I asked Auntie who she was going to vote for. She told me, very seriously, that this was an impolite question. It was a private matter, and I should never ask anyone that question.

I was amazed. Judging from the spirited talk in our kitchen, I would never have thought it was either private or impolite. And further, Auntie continued, she did not vote. Men voted, she added in a tone which suggested that it was improper for women. Like smoking or going into the pool room, even to buy an ice cream cone. I did not tell her that in Chicago, even women smoked.

The summer before the election was my introduction to partisan politics. Contrary to my belief, everyone was *not* a Democrat or a Democrat's friend. One of our neighbors turned on her powerful radio to a thunderous production of the Republican convention. Grandma was indignant, not because it was Republican but because she could not hear her radio preachers on WCFL (Where Christ Flies Low, the announcer explained) or WCBD (Where Christ Blesses Daily). The call letters had impressed me greatly with Christ's power on earth. Even the radio stations were his command.

We surely knew how one neighbor felt about the Democrats, but Grandpa just smiled. Finally, it was election day, and the news stories talked about candidates' last minute messages and predictions, but in truth, getting the results took a long time. Late into the night, Grandpa and I listened, and then he finally said, "Well, they just keep saying the same thing over and over again."

We went to bed, but before we did Grandpa said it would be perhaps two days before we knew for sure. My political choice came from my reliance on Grandpa's judgment. And when the votes were all in and a landslide had been declared, Roosevelt was our new president. But landslide was a fearful word.

"Was there *really* a landslide, Aunty?" I asked.

"That's what they say," Aunty answered, and although I waited, she did not offer an explanation.

Then Aunty and Uncle had company from Chicago who were full of new stories. Roosevelt was a Communist, a Russian, or Rooshan, people said. Or a Socialist. The nice older lady smiled at me and said, "In Chicago, they say NRA stands for Nice . . . Round . . . A." And then she raised her eyebrows and waited for me to laugh. I looked at Aunty, who looked bewildered by her guest. I went down to Grandpa's store and told him what they were saying in Chicago, and he said not to worry about it. And then he gave me a little laugh. Nobody had ever talked like that in Aunty's parlor, and Grandpa knew it.

The elections went on, and on, and then there was that election Grandpa lost. Even the little salary he got was important now, but to Grandpa the people had spoken. He waited, and when election time rolled around again Grandpa was ready, as always, to take his case to the people. I can see him now, dressed up, which wasn't the way I saw him often.

Grandma helped him get ready to go electioneering, wearing his tan suit and his favorite green tie. He would get in the old truck, older every year, that he used to deliver fruit packages, and the old engine would roar to his satisfaction. He would go out to talk to farmers, going from farm to farm. He would respectfully ask for their votes, knowing that some would not be his. People weren't lying, he told me, but only trying to please you.

Election day finally came, and when I got home from school, I told Grandma I was going right down town. After all, the election was right there in Grandpa's store, and I felt entitled to be there. I had watched Grandpa putting the boards together as always, to make the voting booths, and when some lady complained that she wanted more privacy, Grandpa had Aunt Min Phiscator sew some panels to make voting truly secret.

Grandpa saw me come in, and told me I couldn't stay. But, he added, after the polls closed and the votes were counted, I could come down if I would stay out of sight, as much as possible. That was easy, in the big, drafty old building, so I found a chair way to the back, against the partition to the back room. Partially hidden by the voting booths Grandpa would dismantle tomorrow and stack in the basement for next election, I watched the count. Women, who weren't supposed to vote in Aunty's opinion, were sitting at the table along with some men, opening each folded ballot and announcing the votes.

I thought Grandpa's name was called more often than that of his opponent, who had signs printed, an unbelievable luxury. And as the count went on, the smile on his face wavered. He was a nice man, and everyone knew he would have made a good supervisor. But he did not need the job; and everyone knew that Grandpa did. Perhaps that had something to do with the outcome; I do not know.

When I was a little older, I rode on the old truck to deliver cases, and help Grandpa unload them. In the driveway out by the barn, Grandpa's customer said, "Say, Pat, I've wanted to ask you something. I got my assessment, and my taxes are going up again. This isn't easy."

"You're right," Grandpa said, "but I try to be fair. Now you've got this fruity forty acres, one of the nicest farms in the township. And then your neighbor," and I can't remember the name, "has a little less, maybe thirty-six. But he has that creek going all the way through, and a bigger house and barn. Do you think they are worth the same?"

Max Petzke nodded. He understood.

When Grandpa was in his late eighties, he had been visiting his daughter who lived ten miles from him. The day was blizzardy, and roads were reputed to be bad, but Grandpa would not hear of staying one more day. He wanted to go home, right now, and he waited with his overnight case by Aunt Mabel's front door. Out of arguments and patience, my Uncle Will and his son, Bob, negotiated the narrow road between towns.

Uncle Will waited in the car while Bob carried Grandpa's little suitcase onto the porch. But Grandpa did not go toward the house. On the sidewalk, he said, "There's something I want to attend to down the street before I go in the house. You'd better go along home before it gets any later."

Father and son watched Grandpa go down the snowy sidewalk toward the store building with a sign on the door. There was a special school election. And Grandpa had come home to vote.

A Few Good Women

Anne Irgens Vandermolen

She wishes for
a device that will
scrub the toilet without her,
a broom that will
sweep the kitchen without her,
a dust mop that will
wipe the cobwebs without her.

Her children are grown,
her motherhood over,
she suspects that
with such devices,
her husband might choose to
manage without her.

She hires a cleaning service,
a few good women
to scrub, dust, and sweep.
Her husband knows
that in his house
there are still
women at work.

American Male Swings

Joe Bartz

No, he said, I will go again. He pulled twice more on his cigarette, cherishing his resolve, stuffed it out on the dash and hoisted himself out of his '82 Olds hardtop. He hop/limped back across Lake Street, clomped over the low rotting berm of snow-plow and strode, easier now on the soft damp sand, twenty paces south along the street to the old-fashioned swing set the county put up last summer. Again he pumped up until the horizon rose above the ridge bar. The water stretched, an un-January fluid blue-gray; he reached for it with his Reeboks. It was the return of the tentative sunlight that brought him back?

I'd noticed him the first time when, in an unexpected glow of winter sun I looked up from my work and saw one of the swings in motion. I saw the deep bright blue that the classic steel A-frame was painted—the blue that read in the lamp-lit fog last evening but not in this morning's dull overcast. I saw the long, dark-haired man, nearly horizontal at the peak of his arc, in his black togs and bright black and white shoes.

Some minutes later, glancing up at the returned overcast, I saw him smoking in the silver Olds in front of my house. Then another sun-glow and his return to the swing. This time I noticed that he pulled gloves on before he launched himself in the sling seat. People do often stop and park for a few minutes along the beach, sometimes with a take-out lunch or a camera, sometimes in off weather or even in storms. Strollers sometimes stop for a turn or two on the swings. Joggers don't. Three, four, five minutes—I'd gone back to my books—and he was in his car again, smoking again.

Next door the gate banged. Dorothy's physical therapist was leaving. She climbed into a red van, parked in front of the Olds out of my line of sight and I moved to watch her drive off. He didn't rev up and follow, which he would have, unless maybe he knew I was watching, if that had been it. But he didn't. He finished his current cigarette—forty-five seconds?—digesting his high and then pulled out. I watched him for a block and looked back at the swing set. Another guy, adult male, shorter, in a khaki jacket, was swinging, more gently, face to the milky sun and away from the lake. I don't have time for another story, but the swing set's good, the swing set's fine.

My Backyard

Bethany Ann Vizthum

What makes my backyard my special place is because I have fun. These are the things that are in my backyard: a basset hound dog, Charlie, a green hose, a fence, a yellow shed, and a bonfire. My family is there and we're roasting marshmallows.

What else is there? Green grass, dirt, rocks, a wood pile, a small tree, a sand box, flower garden, my swingset, and lots of room to play baseball and football.

My favorite time in my backyard is when my dad, my sister, my brother and I were playing soccer. I was down by the other goal and my dog was in my goal sniffing something. My dad shot the ball in the goal and my dog saved it. He was laying in front of the goal and the ball bounced off him into the bonfire pit. What made it so special was it was so funny.

As you can see, my backyard is nice and big to play in. We have lots of fun back there.

Sturgis Elementary

My Bedroom

Joseph Andrew Biron II

In my bedroom, no one is there with me. I do lots of things in my bedroom. I play on the Sega and with my stuffed animals. When I get the chance, I clean my room. My room is nothing like other ten year olds rooms. I have pictures of Indians and staffs.

Ten weeks ago, something special happened in my bedroom. I was laying down in my bed, and my cat wouldn't leave me alone. I went to my mom and dad. They told me she was in labor. Because a long time ago, we put her outside with another cat, who was a boy. My dad stayed up all night. I went to bed on the couch.

The next morning, I found out the cat had kittens in my bed. Chrissy, the cat, had five kittens. But one suffered and died. So now there are three girls and one boy. I kept sleeping on the couch.

Two weeks later, the cats learned to walk. Three weeks later, they learned to eat. Oh, and was that a mess! Five weeks later, we put the cats outside. Since then, the cats have been living outside and they're fine. We'll have the cats for another four or five weeks.

I didn't really talk about the death of the kitten. When I go into the room, I try not to think about the death of the kitten because when it happened, I cried. I hope the other cats live for a long time. But my room is still special because my cat, my best cat, had babies in it.

Mendon Elementary School

The Park

Brook Yaw

My special place is the park. By the middle school. Where the third grade and fourth graders go. I play and sometimes read. It is fun there. It is also fun when you are sad because you can swing on the swing set. Sometimes I watch the seagles go across the sky. Sometimes I just sit and relax.

Merritt Elementary

Up North

Erik Ivins

When we go up north we camp by a stream. Sometimes I go by the stream and read one or two books before we go mushroom hunting. If it is a hot day out I get to walk in the stream. And when I walk in the stream with a water proof camera I take pictures. I will do this on Memorial Day.

Merritt Elementary

Planting and Celebrating

Lynn Welsch

Just last week, I was looking out my upstairs window down to the vineyard in back of my house. The grapes had just starting blooming. You can only see the flowers if you're looking right at the vines, but the aroma was sweet and fresh and the leaves were a bright new green. As I was looking, I thought about the very first day we worked in those vineyards. We had just lived in Fennville about a month and were trying to get the ground ready to plant our first grapevines. The noise of the tractor was great as I drove! Dust flew around my face and into my eyes. The sun was very hot, and I saw it through a haze as if someone had turned the dimmer switch. My leg was tired from working the clutch and my shoulder was sore from shifting. At that moment I was ready to pack up and move back to Chicago. What was I doing here? I hated this. Starting a business was not what it seemed to be when we first made the decision to move to Michigan. Our dream of starting a winery was still a dream in our minds. No one told me I would be doing all this hard work. I wanted to get to the part where we would be planning, organizing, decorating!

I swallowed hard, and I drove the tractor slowly ahead, while Doug, my husband, followed on foot behind the flat wagon hitched on to the back of the tractor. The field we were in had just been cleared of old, neglected fruit trees. We were picking up the stumps and stones and hauling them away. It was backbreaking work start, jerk (I wasn't a very good tractor driver), climb down, throw stumps on the wagon, climb up again, and take off with another jerk. It took the whole day to clear the field. I was tired, sweaty, exhausted, and sore.

I smiled to myself as I came back to 1998. Just a couple of days ago we celebrated two momentous occasions in our family's history my in-laws' fiftieth wedding anniversary and the twenty-fifth anniversary of the beginning of the winery. To celebrate, we decided to have a moveable feast in the vineyards. All of the family gathered that day. Everyone had fixed a special dish for the dinner. We loaded the food in the special people hauler (sort of a glorified hayrack), everyone climbed on board, and we took off into our 55 acres of grapes. First stop was the Chardonnay vineyards for hors d'oevres and Chardonnay wines. We moved on to the Riesling vineyard, where we had grilled shrimp (my son had taken grills out to the vineyards earlier that day) and dry Riesling. At these two stops the scenery was sweeping. The gentle slope of the vineyards ended at the huge pine stand that is the border of the Todd Farm, famous as the stopping point for Canada geese in the fall. Our next two stops were across the street in the Chardonel for the main course (salmon) and in the Vignoles for dessert (mango burritos). The view in these vineyards was different than the others. The grapes were planted closer together on a flat field, which dropped off to valleys. In one valley was the pond, a favorite swimming place for the dogs we've owned. My son also fished and hunted around that pond before he went off to college.

Over the years I'd taken walks out in the vineyards, and I thought that I had appreciated their beauty, but I looked at the scene in front of me as if for the first time. The trees seemed bigger and the valleys more lush than they had before. With a feeling of surprise, I thought to myself, "I'm living in a place most people come to vacation in because of its beauty." The occasion had something to do with my new outlook, I'm sure the celebration of the past, but also a reminder of a dream we had shared before there were any grapes here when the questions loomed large in our minds, when the future was bright but uncertain. We had built this enterprise together as a family and it was special to see it together. Then later on, my mother-in-law gave me a grape cluster necklace that my father-in-law had given to her 25 years ago when we bought the farm. Tears came to my eyes, and the only thing I could say was, "Thank you." Life affords some moments when you see things clearly and you know you won't forget them ever. This was one of those moments, when you can look back and all the cares and stress of your everyday existence disappear, and the only feeling you have is contentment and a sense of being at peace with your surroundings. When you feel that the risks you took were worth it and that God's hand is always there to grab onto when you stumble. It gives you courage to face the next era of your life.

Venetian Festival

Whitney Schrubba

There are a lot of festivals in St. Joseph. One of them is called the Venetian Festival. The Venetian Festival happens every summer. It is one of my favorites. Also, the food is marvelous.

There are lots of different kinds of food there. My favorite food there is the Elephant Ears. They are so good! They are so big that my sister, my mom, and I have to share one. They also have french fries. My sister likes those the best.

There is music playing all of the time. They have concerts near the beach. I like to listen to the music while eating a hot dog from the Hot Dog Man.

On the beach they have sand sculpting contests. People make lots of different kinds of sculptures. Last year I saw a family making a hot dog with colored water as catsup and mustard.

At Venetian, they also have a carnival with lots of rides. Last year was my first time riding the ferris wheel.

At the end of the last day they have fireworks that light up the night. They're like a bunch of paint cans spilling in the night sky.

If you ever come to St. Joseph in the summer, you should come to the Venetian Festival downtown.

Lincoln Elementary School

Silver Beach

Ann Louise Williamson

The car slows,
swings over to the curb,
A haircut with earrings
leans out the window
asking directions
to Silver Beach.

Silver Beach, my kids
would fist fight
in the back seat, jump
out of the car
before I got the engine off.
They ran on top of the sand
got down on all fours
digging, sand flying
through their legs.
Cute, hairless mutts
I couldn't see
their swim suit bottoms.

Silver Beach, I still go there.
I stay in the car, windows down,
turn off the engine.
The white sails in the water
remind me of mail call
at summer camp, money
sent to grandchildren
in white envelopes.

Taking Back the Past

Christina Phillips

Each weekend, we strolled
to House of David
junior high girls
for strawberry cones
and pony rides,
amusement park
concerts with bearded
long haired men.

Framed postcards
of King Ben.
Rumors lingered
purification rites
and young girls . . .

Purify your blood for Jesus,
Sacrifice anything for true faith
I'll absolve you of my sin.

Now, mummified
in the Crystal Palace,
embalmed by a man
with Egyptian skills
he clasps his hands
across his chest.
Baby pink ribbon
in his long, white hair.

One summer day,
when the park was in a
haze of heat, dressed in white
we posed between the buildings
Jerusalem and Bethlehem.
Somewhere in time, our negative

floated into light,
one picture in a roll that
never developed.

Silver Beach

Reneé White

White wooden beams
    rise up from gold sand
    as if a game of pick-up-sticks became
    well ordered and structured
    providing support for the cars pulled,
    clackety-clack, clackety-clack, clackety-clack,
    to highest point then released to gravity
    plummeting passengers in gleeful terror with
    wind rushing, heart leaping stomach
                              dropping
                                 speed.

Guess your weight! Guess your weight! Step right up!

Carved laughing lady
    bowing with taunting laughter
    loud upon her frozen lips
    unseeing staring eyes in
    nearly wicked painted face.
    A mocking challenge to enter the dark fun
    house with twisting mazes, distorting mirrors,
    rolling barrels and moving floors.

Knock down the milk bottles! Win a prize!

Brass poled carousel
    holding favored white horse in
    jeweled halter, jeweled saddle,
    prancing without motion, ever moving
    yet traveling only to fantasy's destination
    with its eager riders, young and old.

Ring toss, right here! Three tries for a quarter!

Outlined Ferris wheel
    lit like fireflies
    dancing in the night sky,
    reflecting in the water
    couples hoping to be stopped
    at the top
    for a cooling breeze . . . or secret kisses.

Try your strength! Ring the bell!

Penny arcade games
    trinkets often sought . . . seldom won.
    Magnets guided, claws grasping, boxing
    dolls, cycle races . . . games of skill.

Penny pitch! Penny pitch! Step right up! Try your luck!

Sweet smells snake
    through the crowds.
    Pink spun sugar, caramel apples,
    roasted peanuts.

Come in, come in . . . let me tell your fortune, let me read your palm . . .

       while lovers escape the clashing noise to walk along
Silver Beach
    Moonglow working alchemy illusion
    changing sand from sun gold to pewter granules,
    tarnished water to liquid silver,
    sensual in its teasing of the shore . . .
               touching
            retreating
               touching
            retreating.

Soft felt breezes cool hot night,
but not passion,
carry love words from dance hall music . . .
Big Bands . . . "Stardust" . . . "That Old Black Magic"
Bodies move and cast elusive shadows

of unspoken feeling upon the walls.
Lovers playing with the night
exchange promises

    always remembered

        forever forgotten

           Silver Beach and Shadowland

Valentine's Day Dance

Myron J. Kukla

Valentine's Day has always had a special place in my heart among holidays. That's because I learned some very important lessons about life on Valentine's Day many years ago.

One was a lesson I'd never forget: girlfriends cost money.

You have to remember this happened in a time before political correctness; a time before the Equal Rights Amendment; a time before I had a job and money.

I was in the sixth grade and just coming out of that awkward stage where boys think it's fun to show girls bugs and beginning to move into that next stage where guys do other stupid things instead.

There was this girl, Rosemary, who used to wear her beautiful brown hair in ringlets that were popular in the days before styling moosh. I had admired her from afar since we were in the fourth grade. Well, it wasn't that far afar. We sat beside each other in class.

I can remember even now how daintily she ate her crustless peanut butter and jelly sandwiches at lunch, and how amazed I was that anyone could be so neat. I actually had decided in the fourth grade to ask her out, but had waited a few years so as not to appear over-eager.

Our school that year was throwing this big Valentine's Day dance in the gym. It was to be the social event of the season for all the sixth and seventh grades.

Somehow, I managed to talk to Rosemary without a bug in my hand and asked her to the dance. And with the faintest hint of blush on her cheeks, and a demure smile on her face, she agreed.

I was the happiest boy in St. John's School that day. I literally floated home on air, carried by cherubs while Cupid tossed rose-petal hearts before me.

Sauntering into our house, I announced as casually as I could, that I would be going to the school dance on Saturday with Rosemary.

"You're going to have to get her a corsage," said my father, not looking up from his evening paper. "Girls like corsages."

This was something I hadn't planned on. Unwise as I was to the ways of the world, I didn't realize the guy had to pay for the girl's corsage. I just assumed corsages came with the girl. What a dumb system, I thought.

On the day of the dance, I pulled out my life savings of $5.78, which I had put away to buy a pocket knife. "Oh, well, this is for the love of your life," I thought, stuffing the money into my pocket and heading out for the florist shop.

Now I have to say on a scale of 1 to 100 of the most useful things in the world, flowers hadn't ever made my list. Entering the florist shop that day I had no idea of what kind of flower I should buy her. Luckily, the florist seemed to know something about flowers and recommended I buy a red-tinted chrysanthemum with my school's letter on it.

"She'll love it," he advised me. It's a good thing he was there to help, because, left to my own instincts, I probably would have bought her a potted geranium, or a flowering shrub or something.

The corsage cost $2, which was a lot cheaper than a flowering shrub, and I felt pretty good as I headed home with my tissue paper wrapped, red-tinted chrysanthemum in its heart-covered florist box.

Back at home, with all of the naïve delight of a schoolboy, I showed my mother the corsage and she said: "Did you remember to get some candy for her mother? They like that, you know."

It still amazes me that as wise as my parents were in the social graces of the day, it never occurred to them that I had no money to pay for these things.

Trudging down to the local corner store—with the remainder of my pocket knife fund—I bought not one but three boxes of candy. One for Rosemary, one for her mother and one for my mother. I wasn't taking any chances this time, unless the girl's father was owed some sort of Valentine tribute. If so, he was out of luck.

My dad drove me to Rosemary's home to pick her up. I have to say she was a dream in her organdy taffeta party dress, and with as much aplomb as I could muster, I distributed the gifts. I even pinned the corsage to the top shoulder of her dress without causing her any pain.

I'd like to say the evening was a huge romantic success. Actually, for most of the evening, the girls huddled on one side of the gym comparing chrysanthemums while the boys stood on the other side complaining about how much this dance had cost them. It was my guess that this one evening had thrown the pocket knife industry in our town into decline, if not outright collapse.

As the evening wound down to its final dance, I found myself at last alone with Rosemary, dancing to a slow song in a dimly lit corner of the gym. As the strains of the last dance came to an end, Rosemary looked up at me and said "Thank you" and gave me my first kiss.

And at that moment, I learned there were more important things in life than pocket knives.

Marching Music
a sestina

Corey L. Harbaugh

My father loved that marching band
The one my son just watched in wonder
Every year they highlight this parade
The streets and alleys fill
When they march by
Reclaiming the air with familiar music

By the time my mother heard the music
She'd missed the marching band
Waving at dreams, like pageant queens that floated by
So many years left to wonder
How does a lonely life get filled
Who would listen when she prayed

This was my son's first parade
Too young to recognize the music
His baby's senses filled
With the flash and clatter of the marching band
How many years, I wonder
Until to him I'll say goodbye

My father never said goodbye
He slipped into the ranks while we watched the parade
The clues he left made us wonder
Photos, clothes, his favorite music
On the dresser, his wedding band
So many promises unfulfilled

Today these streets are filled
With things I don't want but still buy
The vendors' carts swing heavy with contraband
Beyond their hawking, sounds of a parade
Sirens, whistles, and oh, that marching music
I'm spellbound here, and it's no wonder

From the side of the road I no longer wonder
At how all those ranks got filled
Driven on by marching music
I guess enough has passed me by
That in between the brassy notes of this parade
I hear the steady footfalls of the marching band

Come to attention band, there's no time left to wonder
Fathers watch this parade for gaps to be filled
But I'll keep time when you march by, drive me home with marching music

How to March

Peter Hyland

First
put your feet together
toe to toe
heel to heel

Stand
a string from the top of your head
holds you up
head raised, back straight

Look
not in front of you
but at the tops of trees

Place
one foot in front of the other
heel then toe
rolling on the outside

Act
like you were born
to do only this

St. Joseph High School

Purity Set to Music

Anna Clark

My skin has always been a shade whiter than the others
My head held a little bit higher
My choices already made
I decided I knew the difference between painful and beautiful
I would spend twilights swinging from my magnolia tree
Rocking real hard so the pink-edged petals would rain on me
Myself perfectly matching the chords of Canon in D
so comfortably well
that I believed that
the sound of my laughter
paired with the fragile, unearthly touch of
My Oma's hand
made the song mine only
and though the engulfing scent of grade school
hasn't quite left me yet
I realize all else has
As I now miss twilight to spend time
with my pals from the Breakfast Club
Arguing with my mother
For threatening to throw out my shorts that are
held together by strings and safety pins
More like me than I care to admit
Because though there'll always be
more gossiping, trips to Mickey D's, and football games
It won't be the same since
They uprooted the petal tree
My values did a back-flip
Since my Oma died
And when I think of what chords my life now fits
I can think of the song
But not the title
It must've gone the way of purity,

slipping through the holes between the
strings and safety pins

St. Joseph High School

Brown
(inspired by The Wallflowers' "One Headlight")

Brad Koch

son of the man
Son of that Sam
open me to your way
organ sound like the wind through trees
hallowed, hollowed bellows resonating in their death
two and four slammed to the floor with the force of that pounding snare
hopping bass to skip in the lieu of any understanding
tapping rhythm lost in the verse
found again with Cinderella
electric elegance timed so perfectly
steel string sting in that cold autumn air

raspy voice
son of the man
Son of that Sam
sing now your sweet song of sex
soft sensuality
simple sin

brass slide on that folk guitar
slice through my soul like a dull knife through rotten peach
leave me sad
leave me glad
leave me dead in my tracks

I said son of that man
son yes you can
make me feel real again

St. Joseph High School

Foggy Mountain Breakdown
a sestina

Sherrie Britton

Tonight as I write, I hear my father's banjo,
fast and surprising, like gypsy moths,
as he tumbles out an old bluegrass tune.
He sits across from me at the table
and we talk about fishing and music and dreams
and I can believe he is the man I write

about, but he never really understands what I write,
but thinks it is about his Gibson banjo
and this house where my dreams
are secrets, brown-winged moths
who cannot fly and so land on the table,
wings beating out a silent tune.

Tonight he plays the same tune
and doesn't notice when I write
despite his music, papers spread over the oak table
like a blanket trying to cover this five string banjo
that slowly eats at me, a moth,
keeping me awake, chewing on my dreams.

I try to write last night's dream,
but my pencil can't quite catch the tune.
I try not to notice the luna moth
crawling across everything I write,
reading the alien language of a banjo,
as if it were etched in the lines of the table.

For a moment I forget he is across the table,
remember how my mother told me he used to dream
that he was playing the banjo,
his fingers rumbling across the blankets, imaginary tunes
in his sleep. I know that is how I write,
stories fading in and out like this moth

making his way toward the door, this moth
who turns away, crawls off the end of the table.
I pretend I don't notice, pretend I don't write
for a minute, imagine my dreams
are those muffled, ghostly tunes
spanning this distance between me and a banjo,

or a moth who sees fire in her dreams.
I sit across the table and try not to memorize the tune
he plays over and over. I write a story about a gold-plated banjo.

Dancin' Home in the '60s

Christina Phillips

Vida and I running on skillet
hot sand at Silver Beach.
Minnows in shallow water, ripples
looking for Indian beads to thread.

Floating on mattresses near the pier
til we drifted out.
"Vida, I can't touch bottom!"
Algae wrapping round
our skinny legs
tide pulling us out
undertow waves crashed
over our heads
We fell choking . . .

Stayed up late,
radio tuned to Stevie Wonder.
Vida liked him, so would I.
Who could sleep with people
screaming—
roller coasters down the road.

Mirror maze clown lured us.
I'd get lost. He'd shake
twenty times
laugh "Hee, Hee . . ." into one long
screech
sent me slammin' into glass.

Fun house belly dancer
would tilt our heads
wondering how to swivel metal hips
sexy full circle
all day long . . .

That summer, Vida and I danced upstairs in our nighties,
swiveled, felt the bond
never danced again.

What The Storms Left Behind

Corey L. Harbaugh

> *I should have been born the son of a wolf*
> *Or a bear*
>> *—Edward Hirsch*

Part I.

This slant, gray rain only falls here
In this city. And that wind that mourns
The buildings knows my bones.

From my window at night
I can see broken glass, and it
Looks like fields of diamonds,
Fairy dust, or a yard of fresh snow
Like where I'm from.

Back there God was simpler
Angels were easy to see
Pressed to the plate of church windows
Frozen in paradise
The light passed straight through
Their perfect white wings

Here I have dirty pigeons
And rats that crouch where I won't look
And the husks of cars and people
Abandoned where they quit.

Part II.

I can't remember leaving home
So much as I remember knowing
It was time to go.

After so many nights
At the top end of town
Posing questions to the air.

On those nights when the moon
Was all the sky gave,
And its light filled the fields,
I sprayed the weeds yellow,
Just to hear it drip, rain-like
From the Queen-Anne's Lace.
And then I danced.
The rabbits must have thought I was the son
Of a wolf, or a bear.

But it was those nights watching storms gather
And roll through with a flash and punch,
When warm drops fell straight down,
That my blood learned what the wind carries,
The secret of where storms start.
My skin learned to feel them coming
In the charge and the weight and the depth to the air
My ears could hear cornstalks
Hunkering down in their tedious rows.

And when I was what the storms left behind
I knew the horizon was all I had.

Part III.

I don't know the exact moment I left home
But it must have happened in the silent middle
Of everything happening, like when
A juggler has all three pins in the air
Both hands free, waiting
To catch and throw again

But I'm done apologizing for what I'm not
I know my place in the middle of all this
Somewhere between where I came from
And what I want. Somewhere between

What lightning shows and what the thunder says
I have carved out a certain, easy peace.

So these old buildings and their weather-wrought
Bricks. These dogs that pace empty lots and growl
At shadows,
Are no different than houses in endless rows of
Always been,
Or mutts that squat on neat lawns.

So when the storms come with their stories of home
People hunch and scatter to pull shutters tight
Against them. But not me.
I smell the way the earth waits,
Hear leaves turning on their tender stems
And sleep snug in the gray cradle whisper of the drops
Dreaming of what I left behind.

The Last Bonfire

Grace A. Lucker

My eyes squinted against the sun's rays filtering through the willow trees. In the back field decaying boats in dry-dock, neglect and dry rot eating their hulls, whispered of better summers when fishermen flopped fish on their decks or children dove off their swim platforms.

I fought tears focusing on the scene before me. Turquoise, yellowed-white, and bronze refrigerators stood sentinel around the marina near many of the docks. Ankle high weeds grew where they hadn't been trampled. Sagging docks jutting feebly into the water had boats from the newest to the ones a leak away from joining the shells in the back field bobbing by them.

Near some of the docks, screened lean-tos with dirt floors lent a hobo-camp air to the place. Next to each a stack of wood gathered from the old rotting boats waited for the next bonfire—a fire like none-other. Blues from the bottom paint, purples and greens from engine oil that had soaked into the wood became a rainbow of flames.

The atmosphere and boaters made Whispering Willows Marina special. Everyone was family, no one a stranger, and there was always room at the table for a hungry friend.

Around the bay wisps of smoke from bonfires and grills curled toward puffs of orange and purple clouds. Poignant laughter echoed across the water. The sun slid behind the willows and a soft breeze carried final picnic aromas through the air.

I turned, settling on the bench in front of our bonfire, watching flames lick at hunks of wood. As friends gathered around, beer can tops popped, but an unusual silence hung heavy in the air. This was the last bonfire.

"Hey, why's everyone got such sad faces? We'll all be meeting again," Sonny said, fingering the chain hanging from his belt loop to the huge, probably empty, wallet in his back pocket.

"Sure we will. Maybe we won't be havin' our boats no more, but we won't lose touch." Tom rolled the stub of his well-chewed cigar to the other corner of his mouth, forcing a smile and peeking over smudged glasses.

False bravado. An era ended tonight. When the sun rose tomorrow morning, graders, back-hoes, and bulldozers would turn this haven into a marina most of these boaters couldn't afford.

Baldy ambled up to the fire, popping the top on a Bud. "Hey, I ever tell you folks about how old Gus started this place? Well, he bought this here swamp land down by the river and decided to plant corn. Problem was the birds ate the corn so fast he couldn't harvest it, so he started selling the black dirt. Made a pretty penny too." He took a long swig of beer, eyes darting around to be sure he had everyone's attention, and waiting for the chuckles to die down. "One day a fella came 'round and asked if he could dock his boat over yonder where Gus'd dug out really deep by the river. After that, he said he started digging holes, and folks just wanted to pay him to dock their boats there. So he decided to build them some docks and got some old rubber tires from across the street for boat bumpers so's the boats wouldn't scrape the dock." Baldy rocked back on his heels, rubbing the top of his shaved head, and laughed sheepishly. He rested the beer can on his belly. "Yup, you could tell a boat from 'Gus's Ghetto' by the black smudge marks on their hulls from a mile away."

Doug pitched an empty into the back of his nearby pickup and reached for another. "I remember the winters the ice got so thick it raised the docks up. Old Gus decided if he greased the pilings the oil wouldn't let the ice stick. Of course, all the boats had grease on them, and the DNR got on him for pollution." Laughter rippled around the fire as the last rays of sun painted the clouds a brilliant purple. "Hey, George, remember when he got you to help him with that dock hoist?"

George pulled out a knife and started cleaning his nails. "He knew I was a good mechanic. We got this old dump truck and welded a boom off the front bumper with a cable hooked from the bed to the boom. When he lifted the bed of the truck, like to dump it, the cable would pull up the boom and he'd set and pull docks with that invention. It was something. He called it Hitler. We should have patented that idea."

"And I remember when they tore down the Napier bridge. Gus bought up some of them girders and put them together." Tom squinted against the cigar smoke curling in his eyes. "Then he bought the old elevator motor out of the Whitcomb Hotel. He rigged it to them girders, figuring he could use it as a boat hoist. Trouble was, the motor went so fast it belly flopped them boats in the water so hard it, bout busted the planks off the ribs." Once again laughter rippled through the group, the multicolored flames from the fire lighting their faces.

"Yup, old Gus was something all right." Sam rolled back on his heels and winked at me. "If ya wanted any repair work done on your dock or anything, all ya had to do was send your wife or girlfriend over to ask him, and by golly, before you knew it, the job was done. I waited two months one year to get some electric to my dock 'til I finally got a gal to go out with me. Course she only lasted a week, but I finally got that electric to my dock."

"Yeah right, and that's probably all you got." Doug threw a couple more old boards on the fire. "I'll never forget the first boat I bought. It was from Gus. I was fresh out of college and had just started teaching. He started to put it in the water with that hoist of his, and I saw a hole in the bottom. I told him about it, he shrugged, picked up a stick, and whittled at it a while, then stuck it in the hole. I ran that boat for two years without a bilge pump or a leak."

Harry snagged his arm around Gloria's neck. "Then there was that spring he'd fixed up one of them boats back in the field. Worked on it all winter as I remember. Some folks came in looking to buy, and he sold it to them for seventeen hundred dollars and rented them a dock for the season. They never did pay him a dime for the boat. Next year he sold that same boat all over again. Don't recall how many times he sold that boat or if he ever got any money for it, but he always got his dock rent."

"First time I ever saw Gus he was driving around in this old dump truck. It had a pile of dirt in the back with a tree growing out of it that must have been ten feet tall." Gloria sipped from her plastic glass of wine. "And I always knew where to find Harry on a Saturday afternoon in the winter."

"Sure, I'd finish your honey-do list, grab a six pack, and head down to Whispering Willows. Gus always had a fire stoked in the salamander to cut the chill. He had the greatest workshop in that place and his overstuffed easy chair. We'd stand around drinking beer and telling stories all afternoon—mostly lies I suppose, but we had a great time." Harry rubbed the cold can of beer across his brow. "They'll probably tear that down too."

The silence hung heavier than the September air that night, broken only by popping boards in the fire.

"He'd drive around the place like a king surveying his kingdom at about two miles an hour with his arm hanging out the window." Tom cleaned his smudged glasses on his shirttail only smearing them more, but I suspected he was keeping tears at bay. "Always had a dumb nickname for everyone too. Like 'Badly,' 'Long-hair,' 'Whistle-Dick,' 'Widerwoman' . . . ."

"He always had a saying for everything, too. Told me once Jesus was a Methodist, cause he used every method he could to convert people." Sonny added, "When they told him what a dump this place was and to clean it up, he just shook his head and said the spirit was willing but the flesh was weak."

"I was having problems getting the dry rot out of my hull and new planks back in one spring. Gus just slapped me on the shoulder and said, 'You know, Brother Douglas, paint covers a multitude of sins.'" Doug's imitation of Gus's German accent sent a ripple of laughter through the crowd.

"Well, I gotta go, my Billy'll be waiting up for me. Maybe she'll give me some sugar tonight." Baldy tossed his beer can into the fire.

"Geez, Baldy, that's a ten-center—and mine too." Doug grabbed a stick and started digging the can out of the fire. Everyone erupted in laughter.

"You skinflint fool. All these years I thought you was dead broke, hanging on to every Michigan ten-center like it was gold and driving that old-beat up black pickup. Then one day you pulled up in that big old fancy boat from your high flalootin' marina downstream. I thought you'd borrowed it from someone till you told me it was yours. Guess you never was too good to come stand around the fire and drink with us after you left outa here, was ya."

Doug looked down at the fire then straight into Pollock's eyes. "I may have gone elsewhere because this place was sold, but we can't have bonfires down there. The lawn is mowed, great docks, and the boaters are nice, but it's just not the same."

"Ya mean ya have to behave respectful like." Sonny pranced around like a dandy.

"I guess, but I could always come back here and let my hair down." Doug threw Sonny another beer. "Remember that's my ten-center."

Sonny sauntered over to me. "You're awful quiet tonight, missy. Ya okay?"

I choked back tears. "I'm fine, Sonny. Can I ask a favor?"

"Anything you want, missy."

"Can I have this bench I always sit on, you know, to take home with us to sit on around the fire in the back yard. It won't be the same, but, you know. . . ."

"Ya, young un, I know. Sure, you take it. And the first bonfire you all have you better invite us out to join ya, ya hear?"

"I hear."

Bonfires grew dim around the marina and head-lights illuminated the dirt road toward Niles Avenue. Good-byes echoed around the marina with promises of getting together over the winter and fishing together next spring.

Today when I drive through Eagle Point Marina, I have to admit it is beautiful. Asphalt roads, fiberglass docks, and cleanliness abound. There's even a clubhouse and a swimming pool. Where kids perched on rocks, dangling their feet in the river hoping for a big fish to snag their hook, a row of modern houses sit. Condominiums are where the old boats rotted waiting for a discerning eye to see a treasure to restore.

There'll never be another Whispering Willows with its down-home camaraderie, bonfires, and multicolored refrigerators. Some say cleaning up such a blight on the community was a blessing. But they missed the real blessing. I guess as long as we remember Gus, the gang, and the fun, Whispering Willows Marina will never die.

We never did have everyone over for a bonfire. But I still sit on that bench every fall by our fire in the back yard after pulling our boat for the season. The grandkids cuddle with me and listen to Doug tell stories about Gus, Sonny, Tom, Baldy, and Whispering Willows—and I remember.

The Red Brick Road

Elizabeth Haines

My earliest indication of the world and its wonders came in books. The village of Galien in which I grew up, maintained its brick Main Street while surrounding towns covered their uneven roads with asphalt. If you followed the red brick road to the edge of town, you found passage to both the familiar and the exotic. At the edge of town, stood the library.

Within the library's walls, I traveled far. I followed Dr. Seuss down Mulberry Street and Dorothy to the Emerald City. Later, I trailed Jane Eyre to Thornfield Hall with our garage standing in as that great house. I read Nancy Drew and assumed treasure awaited the observant beneath the lilac bushes, or in my father's cigar boxes and my grandparents' attic. I imagined myself with English children who used torches instead of flashlights, but who climbed trees just as I did. Less familiar places and less familiar times intrigued me the most. I didn't grow up in the South or in King Arthur's time or live at a boarding school, but I imagined I did. I washed the dishes and pretended I worked as a scullery maid in a castle. At a moment's notice, my brother and I could be the sheriff and deputy hunting down the wily escaped prisoner played by our not always so eager sister. Sometimes we looked for footprints and tracked what would surely turn out to be the Abominable Snowman through the snow in the back yard.

As I grew older, I wandered between the shelves in the library and began to dream of creating my own stories. I loved to read, but I knew early on that I also wanted to write. What exotic lands my characters would visit, what escapades they'd enjoy!

While I looked harder and harder for adventure, I took for granted all the familiar things I did during childhood: catching fireflies at dusk, the corn and sausage roasts with the neighbors, trick-or-treating with our cousins, rubbing my fingers against a frosty pane of glass until I could see the school bus approaching, and whispering with my little sister while we waited for Christmas morning. Where was the adventure in that? I longed to cross the ocean, appear on television, and be a writer.

It's taken time, but now I've been a foreign exchange student to the Netherlands, appeared as a contestant on a game show, and best of all, had a short story accepted for publication. The writing is my enduring delight, the dream that survived everything else. None of my other great adventures appear in my mystery writing. Instead, it is the familiar about which I write.

Now, I live in another small town with my husband. We have a library on the town square, a Fourth of July parade, a notice board at the grocery store, Boy Scouts selling wreaths door to door, and if the wind is just right, we can sometimes hear the marching band practicing at the high school. It is exactly the sort of town in which my characters live.

My townspeople find clues to the mystery at Halloween parties, or overhear a vital bit of information at the corn and sausage roast, they listen to the band playing and wonder whatever happened to poor Mrs. Grayson. And I always send them down the red brick road to the library at the edge of town.

After all, it's where things begin to happen.

Hot, Humid Halls

Nikki

It's finally here,
the end of school.
I can't wait,
it'll be so cool.
No more walking
through the hot, humid halls,
No more answering
when the teacher calls.
No more sitting
through boring classes,
No more using my agenda
like hall passes.
The one thing I'll miss
is all of my friends.
I hope I'll see them
after school ends.
Then next year when we return,
as the "seniors" of the middle school.
All the seventh graders will look up to us,
thinking—no, *knowing* that we rule!

Gull Lake Middle School

One Violet Spring

Mary Alaniz

Kindergarten didn't exist in rural Michigan in 1945 when I was four-years-old, so my parents expected to send me to school when I was six-years-old to begin first grade. However, all I could think about at the age of four, was school. I couldn't wait to start! Books were treasures to me, and I longed to have workbooks with blanks to be filled, such as my older brothers brought home from the one-room rural Imber School[1] which they attended. I pleaded and begged to go to school, so when winter began to ease in early 1946, my mother talked with Mr. Bonfiglio, my brothers' teacher, about my visiting school for a few days. He agreed, not knowing that he had acquired a permanent student. My visiting became a daily routine, and I became a member of the first grade class.

No one could possibly know how I loved that school and everything associated with it. I loved the physical building. It was a plain white structure, and to the right of the door in the entryway were hooks for hanging coats. To the left of the door in the entry way was a table which held a bucket and dipper for getting a drink and a sandwich toaster which we used for noon lunches. During lunch, when Mr. Bonfiglio wasn't looking, the older boys would press the lid of the toaster down hard with their hands so that the sandwiches came out paper thin. Mr. Bonfiglio warned us that eating those thin sandwiches would cause ulcers, but I remember actually liking my peanut butter sandwiches done in that manner. My brothers always traded their peanut butter sandwiches with our classmates, Joel and Bertha Sullivan, for their thick ham sandwiches spread with lard and nestled in large homemade biscuits.

In the front of the actual school room was a large wood burning stove, a piano, and a recitation table where individual classes were held. Each heavy wooden desk in the room had an ink well, and the entire front wall was covered with blackboards.

There were no inside bathroom facilities, but even this didn't bother me, because the girls' outhouse was filled with antique pictures, discarded from some-where. They were stacked on the floor, and the oak frames were large and heavy with elaborate golden ornamentation. Every time I made a trip there, I laboriously

---

[1]The Imber School was located in Batavia Township in Branch County, Michigan.

moved each picture to look at *Washington Crossing the Delaware* and at elaborately dressed men and women with serious faces staring out at me. Evidently my bathroom trips were rather lengthy, because one day Mr. Bonfiglio asked me what took me so long, and I explained that I always took time to look at the pictures. This explanation must have satisfied him, because he never questioned me again, and I continued looking at the pictures during bathroom visits.

Not only did I love every aspect of that wonderful old school building, but I very much loved my teacher, Mr. Bonfiglio. His study for the priesthood at Notre Dame University had been interrupted by the war, and according to the stories I overheard from knowing adults, the war had left him rather shaken, and he felt that a year spent teaching in the pastoral setting of the Imber School would be healing.

I thought Mr. Bonfiglio was the most handsome man I had ever seen. He had black wavy hair and an olive complexion and wonderful hands with neatly manicured fingernails. I loved to watch his hands as he played the piano or followed a written line in a book with his fingers, and I felt that Mr. Bonfiglio loved me also. Never did he utter an unkind word to me, and he sincerely praised my achievements. He started me with the first graders when I entered the school, and I was soon reading, adding, and printing. I thought our readers were beautiful. I don't recall the name of them, but they were pre-*Dick and Jane* and had hard black covers with narrow green and orange stripes.

Not only did I love my assigned lessons, but I also thoroughly enjoyed listening when the older students had geography and history classes at the recitation table, and sometimes Mr. Bonfiglio let me use the wooden history question box with the older students. In the box were questions which Mr. Bonfiglio and the older students wrote on slips of paper. Answers were on the back of the slips of paper, and students questioned one another using them. It was from the history question box that I first learned about Balboa, Cortez, Lewis and Clark, and Amerigo Vespucci. At other times, Mr. Bonfiglio had me work with Billy, an eighth grader who had difficulty reading. We would use the first grade reader, and Billy would read to me, and Mr. Bonfiglio taught me how to help Billy sound out words which he did not know.

Sometimes during recess, my friends and I would stay in, and Mr. Bonfiglio would play the piano, and we would sing. He also talked to us about artists, so I began going through magazines every night and cutting out pictures I thought he would like. I don't know if he particularly appreciated the art I brought each day, but he mounted every picture I took to him, on the wall, and this encouraged me to search even harder for pictures I thought he would like. I remember one night finding a picture of a beautiful woman in a silky white slip standing against a sky of midnight blue. I thought the picture was lovely, but my mother felt it was not appropriate to take to school. I was looking only at the aesthetic quality of the picture, and, at the time, didn't realize that it was an advertisement for a specific brand of women's underwear. I don't remember if the picture made it to school or not, but I know I tried to convince my mother that Mr. Bonfiglio would appreciate the picture for its beauty, just as I did.

Not only did I love the school building, my teacher, and every lesson presented, I also loved the rustic, wooded setting of The Imber School, and when spring came that year, it was like the dawning of creation to me. In back of the school was a small stream and beside the school was a narrow lane. Cowslips bloomed in the stream, and each noon we walked down the lane with our lunches to sit on rocks, fallen trees, or the ground to eat. We were surrounded by blue and yellow violets, adder's tongue, Dutchman's breeches, and trilliums. I was awed by the pastoral beauty and gently warmed by the spring sun. We found polliwogs, frogs, toads, snakes, and turtles and picked bouquets of flowers which Mr. Bonfiglio put in jars and set on the window sills. I loved stepping from stone to stone in the stream and looking at the vegetation and stones, bright beneath the water.

School buses were nonexistent at that time, so I walked the two miles to and from school every day. I loved to walk. In the morning, mothers were often on the porches or in the yards seeing their children off to school, and nearly every day I joined friends on the walk. My brothers had old bicycles which they usually rode, but my mother always asked them to stay with me on the route to and from school. I could have ridden on the back of one of their bikes, but I preferred walking with my friends, so I continually slowed down their bike riding as they tried to monitor my whereabouts. At that age I had absolutely no sense of time, and I visited with any neighbor who happened to be out. One morning, we were evidently late, and my brother Blaire was trying to ride slowly enough on his bike to stay near me. I, however, had stopped to talk with Mrs. Pierce who was in her yard and ignored his calls telling me to hurry. Finally he turned around and roughly picked me up and put me on the back of the bike. The ride to school was fast and frightening. I hung on tightly to my brother's back, and by the time we arrived at school, I was in tears. Mr. Bonfiglio was upset when he saw I was crying and asked for an explanation. Never did I come out a winner at that age when there was a controversy with my older brothers, but that day was a singular triumph for me, because after hearing my explanation, Mr. Bonfiglio kept my brother at the blackboards that morning writing over and over, "I will not tease my little sister and make her cry."

Usually the walk home from school was more relaxed with no one hurrying me, and my brothers didn't feel compelled to watch me as closely as they did in the mornings. Along the route was an abandoned house, unique, because it was a rather sound structure and the owner had simply walked out one day leaving it completely furnished and intact. The grass was tall, and tiger lilies and lilies of the valley grew in the yard, and on many afternoons, when my brothers and their friends were out of sight, my friend Bertha and I scrambled to the front porch to gaze in the windows. What fascinated me most were the magazines and newspapers still open on the stands beside chairs. I often heard my parents talk about the owner who had supposedly moved to Chicago, and although I never saw him, I had a sinister picture of him in my mind and always felt that some day he would come around the house and catch us peering in his windows. I was not frightened enough, however, to stop the ritual of walking up on his porch and looking in on a part of life to which I could add my own fantasies.

As spring began to ripen into summer that year, we celebrated the last day of school with a picnic in the school yard attended by parents and younger brothers and sisters. I did not know at the time that the lovely green and white innocence of my childhood had drawn to a close. School would never be held again at the Imber. The door was locked that day, and the school stood abandoned for a number of years until someone bought it and carved it into a house. I don't believe I ever saw Mr. Bonfiglio again, although I do know that he did not return to the priesthood but became a high school English teacher and died too young.

The next year, as I entered the second grade, rural schools fell victims to the consolidation process, and I, along with the other rural children, became subjects of modern school systems. We exchanged walks in the fresh air for smelly school busses, we exchanged classic reading books for *Dick and Jane*, we exchanged cottage-like wooden school houses with wooden walls and wooden floors for brick, concrete and formica, we exchanged cool drinks from a dipper in a pail of water for more healthy drinks of tepid water from dirty drinking fountains, we exchanged long, lazy noon hours under the sun and among the flowers for hot cafeterias where the end of the noon hour was rudely punctuated by a shrill bell rather than by the call of a teacher. In the name of progress, we exchanged the sublime and the majestic Thoreau-like atmosphere where learning exuded from every aspect of one's surroundings for a structured, more accurate precise atmosphere which the czars of education had decided was best for innocent young children.

No Song to Sing

Kitty Wunderlin

The old school bell hangs silently without its rope,
Only the wind will ring it now
And who will hear it, but a lonely cow
Grazing where the dawdlers ran when late for school.

The meadows green and lush with dew and rain and sun
Are shaded by the silent trees, so tall and old.
Trees canopy across the dusty, gravel road
Lined by weathered fences, long since yielding to a child's leap.

All around the red brick school the weeds grow high
Arching thorns now clutch the handle of the door
As in the fairy tales from days of yore,
They lock the sleeping princess in.

The hazy, late-summer sun slants down on dusty seats
And flickering, softened shadows play on wall and door
While books, their precious pages brown with age, lay strewn upon the floor.
There lingers in the silence . . . Learning's whispered hush.

Laughing, golden autumn leaves may invite us there,
But gone are the sweet young faces, gone their morning-bright shine
Gone are the one room schoolhouse and the music of murmured lines.
It has no renaissance to bring and it has no song to sing.

Milton Street

Ron Weber

We're lucky we didn't break our legs
Jumping from the porch;
What do children know of luck.
Days of play were all we knew,
    all that mattered.

Remember the wild berries we
Picked along the fence for
Pies our mothers would make? Strange
Their smiles in summer-heated kitchens,
But the hard part was the picking,
    we were certain of that.

We watched the welders in the
Factory across the street
Fascinated by their eerie
Metal masks and
Copying them with sparklers
On the Fourth of July.
Curious to us why they would
Leave such fun so rapidly
At the end of the afternoon.

The old vacant lot is asphalt
Now; cars replaced the weeds.
That tall grass hid our
Adolescence then as we
Reclined to watch the sky
And spoke of serious things,
Asking questions we couldn't answer.
Understanding was in silent moments,
    the unsure touching.

I know now why they left
So rapidly, but I haven't
Watched many clouds glide by
Nor sipped the brandy of sunset
As it spills across the sky.
I haven't lain in tall grass since,
Have you?

The Clouds

Beth Aven

I look up and see the world ahead of
me.
Flinging up and then thrusted up
again to see their faces.
Giggling voices surrounded my
seemingly weightless body.
They appear to be enjoying the same
flight as I.
Their glowing faces then show
themselves again.
I peer at their sweet childish figures;
I smile at the laughing
clown that suddenly appears. I
glance over at the words
'Eagle Lake Elementary' and I
wonder what it will be like without
those
familiar words hovering around in
my youthful mind.
I turn to my right and a little girl
calls my name saying,
"Time to go in now Beth!"
Will I ever grow up?
I again look up into the heavens and
I whisper to myself,
"Not likely!"

Edwardsburg Middle School

Where Am I From?

Anne L. Lape

Watch my hand and imagine
that my fingers are technicolor beaches
The surrounding air
Kaleidoscope lakes
Nails pictured rocks
Veins highways
My summer tan the sunset, the sand,
and a single loon.

A Soul's Images

Jennifer S. Baggerly

I am from . . .

oiled wooden floors, chili in pots, ebony carvings from Nigeria, the picture of the courthouse when it burned, coffeepots that perk on the stove, uneven sidewalks broken by the maple tree roots, and gathering paper thin snail shells and bouquets of violets from the river bank.

I am from . . .

Coty loose powder, bath size bars of Zest, Green Excedrin bottles filled with broken pieces of chalk, elastic button bracelets, Butter Rum Life-Savers, and orange circus peanuts secretly eaten before breakfast while watching cartoons on Saturday morning.

I am from . . .

a John Deere 4020 that Grandpa and I took down the lane, deer at dusk eating the new corn, knowing everyone on Snow Prairie Road, Brach's chocolates sold by the pound only during winter—it melts in the summer, and scrapbooks filled just for me, with images from calendars and magazines held in place with Elmer's School Glue.

I am from . . .

breath that smells like coffee and cigarettes, hard-working hands that never come clean, drainage ditches, iodine for cuts, poison ivy, grapevines tangled in the Sycamore limbs, stone piles, and electric wire fences to hold the horses.

I am from . . .

a green Dodge pickup with a homemade bed of wood because the first rusted away, a brown Buick with a "go to hell" light, oily patches where diesel fuel spilled, and hay lofts where kittens and raccoons were born.

I am from . . .

the hole in the barn through which Grandpa drove a tractor, woodchucks that crawled into irrigation pipes and died, a corn picker that grabbed

and tore away my Grandpa's right hand, popping popcorn on the stove
and lifting the lid to shower the kitchen, and mercury lights that
illuminate the farm at night.

I am from . . .
   images of the past that ground and nourish my soul.

Horse Trained

A. James DeFields

The years of the Great Depression were memorable years. . . . There were only a few cars polluting the air and in the area in which I lived horses were still used for farming.

As a young farm boy, I was fascinated by our horses. It always seemed so wondrous that something so big could be controlled and used by mere man. At first we had two horses. One was a white mare named Queenie and the other a bay gelding named Joe. Joe was blind. Whenever Dad went into the horse barn he would speak to Joe so that he would know we were there.

Dad often let me curry the horses—it made me feel all grown up. One day when I was about seven, I decided to curry Old Joe when Dad had Queenie out in the field cultivating corn. Picking up the curry comb and brush, I stepped into Joe's stall and laid my hand on his back. Joe kicked so hard that he took a big gouge out of the side of his stall, missing me by just a frog's hair. Of course I yelled in surprise and Old Joe calmed right down. After that I too always spoke to him before I entered his stall.

Another time while I was currying Joe, he kept pushing against me, squeezing me against the side of his stall. I poked him with the handle of the brush and he reluctantly moved over, then he stepped back toward me with his front hoof, planting it right on top of my bare foot. I pushed on him, poked him with the handle of the brush, yelled and pleaded with him but he wouldn't move. Finally, after about five minutes (it seemed like an hour), he moved his hoof and at the same time he turned his head toward me and let out a big horse laugh. I didn't realize it until later, but that darn horse did it on purpose, as proven by the fact that he had put just enough weight on my foot to keep me from pulling it out from under his hoof. The foot wasn't even bruised.

Somehow, I never had a warm feeling for Queenie like I had for Joe, maybe because Joe was blind or because Queenie was used for most of the single horse work and not around the barn as much.

I have to give Queenie a lot of credit though because she seemed to understand about Joe being blind. She started giving a whinny any time one of us entered the horse barn. I know she was doing it to warn Joe, because she never did it if Joe wasn't in his stall. When harnessed as a team, Queenie always assumed the role of the lead horse, which made it a lot easier for Joe, as well as the driver.

I started working one horse at a time in the fields when I was eight. I was so small, Dad had to harness the horse for me. I couldn't manage to lift the harness up onto the horse until I was nearly ten.

Mostly, I liked working Old Joe best, because he moved slow and steady and responded immediately to spoken commands. The only time I needed to use the reins was to get him lined up with a row.

Queenie was the first one to die. She broke her leg trying to climb a cherry tree to get the cherries. Dad had to shoot her. We buried her up on the hill where she could look out over the whole valley. We never replaced Queenie.

Old Blind Joe got too old to work when I was nine and we retired him to his own nice pasture with his own door into the horse barn so that he could go in and out of the weather whenever he liked. When he died of old age a few years later, we buried him next to Queenie on top of the hill.

In the meantime, Dad had purchased a western mare. We knew she was western, because she had three or four different brands on her left hip. We named her Belle, but we should have named her Mule, Bullhead or Pighead, because she was the most stubborn, obstinate, tenacious and self-willed horse with whom I ever came in contact. Finally however, we came to a working relationship—we just gave in and let her do things in her own way.

One of the most irritating things that she did was to stop whenever she came to the end of the field or end of the row. She would stop and rest almost exactly 30 seconds each time and then start up on her own. At first, we tried everything to get her to move before she was ready: slapping her with the reins, using a whip and even getting in front of her and pulling on her bridle. Nothing worked. And like I said, we finally gave up and did it her way.

Another of her idiosyncrasies was that she refused to be hooked up to any farm implement after being taken out of the barn, until she had a drink of water. At that time we had dammed up a small creek near the barn. The dam made a little pond about five or six feet square and about a foot and a half deep. The pond was down slope from the barn and Belle always took off for the pond at a dead run and if it had been raining would arrive at the pond with all four feet sliding. That horse was so pigheaded that even if I took her to the pond for water, then took her back into the barn to put the harness on, she would still take off for the pond at a dead run, when I took her back out of the barn.

The hill on our farm was and was about a mile long. I often rode Belle bareback and especially liked to run her that half mile along the ridge of the hill. One sunny afternoon, right after a nice warm summer rain, I decided to go for a ride. I had watered all the animals at noon, so didn't think she would need to be watered. I mounted her while she was still in her stall, as I could put a foot into the side of her stall in order to climb aboard. Otherwise, I would have had to find a box or crate to stand on.

Ducking my head way down, I backed Belle out of the stall and rode her out of the barn. Unfortunately, I did not keep a tight grip on the reins. She jerked her head down, tearing the reins from my hand and took off at a dead run down the slope toward the pond. She gained considerable speed down the slope and came to a sliding stop at the edge of the pond. However, I did not stop until I landed in the middle of the pond with a loud splash.

Feeling stupid and inadequate, I crawled out of the pond thinking "Thank God no one was around to see my humiliation!" But, wouldn't you know it? I looked toward the house and there was my mother, bent over with laughter. That night I really took a ribbing.

The summers are a blur for the next few years. World War II came, I went to high school, discovered girls, went into the Navy and grew up. I had no time to think of horses.

Now, in my sunset years I often think of my beginnings. Invariably I end up thinking of Old Blind Joe and Queenie. I can see them standing side by side on top of the hill, small white clouds racing across a vivid blue sky, their manes and tails standing out in the wind and if I listen closely, I can faintly hear them whinny, urging me to come join them.

Paint Horses

Jessica M. Buckingham

Paint horses
lying there in
the green
grass in silence
with a
calm breeze,
whistling right above
their baking
bodies
in the sun
like cookie sheets
full of chocolate
chip cookies,
with little fear
in their eyes.

Centreville Junior High School

cows outside my window

Andrew Woolf

As I woke up I screamed,
"mom there are cows outside my window"
I thought that
I was dreaming
but then mom asked,
"what kind of cows dear?"
I said, "cows . . .
cows with black spots . . .
cows I see at the dairy farm."
As I got out of bed
I said,
"there are **milk** cows outside my window."
But they must be flying
because I'm on the second floor.
I said,
"mom the cows . . .
The cows are **flying** around my window"
My mom

being the way my mom is
said, "just go back to bed dear."
then I fainted
but really I woke only up
to the smell
of my mom cooking breakfast.

Gull Lake Middle School

Casino

Todd Thiel

small, brown, scratched hands
pulling the slot machine handles
he imagines that he's in Las Vegas
but he's at Adams Park pulling sticks off oak trees
"Why are you killing them?" I ask.
He says, "At least I win the money."

Centreville Junior High School

Ode to Mrs. Weatherbee's Automatic Sprinklers

Tiffany L. Troyer

Perched at the top of our hill,
Sitting on my favorite bike,
Purple with pink handlebars
That have shiny aerodynamic pom-poms
Which help me gain speed to attack the enemy.
I push off, peddling hard.
Small pieces of gravel and dry leaves
Crunch beneath my tires.
Rushing past our house,
Then the neighbors'.
The homes hold the injured soldiers,
No longer able to fight.
Then to Mrs. Weatherbee's
Where sprinklers, the enemy, launch droplets of water at me.
Krrrrrsplat! Like bombs and musketballs they attack me,
Shooting me,
Trying to knock me down.
I pass through the drenching water,
It takes only a moment,
Then pull on to Mill Street at top speed,
Circling the short bumpy road,
Then into the overgrown field
By the building that used to be Denton Mills.
My bike slows to a stop
In the waist high weeds
That conceal the remains of my fellow soldiers,
Not strong enough to survive.
I turn around
And start the hard climb
Uphill on our gravel driveway, then,
As I pull around the curve,
I am back to the sidewalk
To start the battle again

Well into the darkness of night,
Until the enemies are defeated
And Mom calls me in for bed.

Centreville Junior High School

Coming Home to an Empty House

Ian McLaren

I approach the empty house
nothingness setting in on me;
my sister at the table
intensely coloring;
but only in my mind

I walk to the couch
nothingness hangs around me;
my dad in the chair
reading the paper;
but only in my mind

I lie down
nothingness droops over me;
mom at the stove
making dinner;
but only in my mind

I wait
seems like hours
but only minutes;
waiting
waiting

phone rings
mom
on her way home

nothingness
will soon end.

Gull Lake Middle School

Headquarters, Where Your Heart Is
(For my brother, Bill)

Mary Ann Wehler

Hello, calling Headquarters! This is Bill—Do you hear
me? Come in! Come in! At my parents' farm, brother
Bill strung his walkie talkie from a blanket tent to the house,
a call to mother, *Do you hear me?* He played cars under

the dining room table, used the rungs for roads. The only
time I knew he existed was when I tripped over his toy
jeep in my heels. On my way to a dance or party, I'd
scream, *Mom, if I break my neck, you'll be sorry!*

Last night, I talked to Mom, she's 95. Every day's call
starts with *How was your day?* Her days are spent in bed.
She says, *Not so good.* Thank god, Bill had been there.
He's 60 now. She starts to cry, tells me the washing

machine's broken. *I told him to cut off my nightgown. He*
wouldn't. She doesn't want to say she lost control of her
bowels. *He had to scrub the carpet. Mary Ann, he never*
saw me naked before. He went to the Laundromat. I'm

wearing a diaper. What a mess! Her voice is shaky and
weak. I call the airline, get a reservation for as soon as
possible. Do you hear me? Do you hear me? I need to get
to Headquarters. It's in Florida now. Mom, Mom, Mom . . .

No Mountain

Norma Strong

when the mountain
looked for me

i was landlocked
in michigan

among great cold lakes
feeding off trout & walleye

hiding in fields of corn
spread like melted butter

among the hills
watching white owls

in red barns
fly among cobwebbed rafters

once in Canton

Jeremy Schnotala

I remember life being a soybean field oasis,
    a dirt road paradise amidst
    a cement labyrinth.

Living in crayfish creeks and
    cornfield forts and bat infested
    attics

Hearing the plowed down
    root cellar shout
    leave me alone, where's the beef,
    and take the pepsi challenge.

I come from the father
    who hunts for flying squirrels
    and starlit nights
    and hunts for skinks and salamanders
    and ancient fishing holes but who
    never hunts for me

I come from the tired woman
    who drives buses and cleans
    houses and who leaves hidden
    notes and scriptures and hopes
    and peanut butter sandwiches
    in crumpled bags long before
    we wake and who finally
    went to her room one
    day and closed her door and
    slept alone for fourteen months

I remember life being a lost lonely
    silo that stands amidst
    the rubble of a tornado
    blown barn

And I know that I will one day
    go back there
    and hide forever

Depression

Coral J. Fry

Depression
yanks you by the shirt collar,
pulls you up, nose to nose, teeth clenched,
spits in your face, "Watch this!"
Slams you down on the sofa.
Then, with its knee on your chest,
injects poison into your brain
and cuts your legs off, cleanly,
    so there is no blood
    and no way to leave.

kite season

Jeremy Schnotala

it means dads and sons
        and fun

I made one once
from cereal boxes
and stolen sticks
        from the neighbor boy's
        perfect family

I wanted to set his on fire
        but then who'd
        buy him stuff
        that I could
        Pick through like
        Cinderella
        when it's trashed

I did buy a spool of
        string once from money
        mom gave me to buy
        away my hurt

But of course my kite
wouldn't fly

It was too heavy
with me

But I ran through the
        field anyway
        stepping on dirt clumps
        and young soybean plants

my string tied to the wind
pulling me away from it all

October

Sharon Bippus

The geese are flying overhead,
Forming elegant geometric patterns,
Moving like synchronized swimmers.
They know the cold is coming.

The potted flowers on the porch
Won't last much longer.
I can't keep hauling them in at night.
A hard frost will take them soon.

The marigolds out front are curling brown and tight.
Under the gray afternoon sky I harvest them for seeds,
Pinch off their tops, pop them into a paper bag.
Back in the house, my fingers hint of them for hours.

After dinner we walk in the dark,
Past houses lit with Halloween lights,
The concrete under our feet
Soft with layers of leaves.

The geese are overhead.
Invisible, moving in the night.
I wonder what they share,
Where they go.

Fun on the Nineteenth Hole

Davey Robison

At Cedar Lake I grab a pin out of my bag and a ball
Dad watches me as I prop the ball on the pin
I stretch before I hit the ball because I don't want to pull a muscle.
I take a deep breath now, ready to hit the ball.
With a quick smooth motion of my arms the ball is sent flying
250 easy
Walking to my ball, I'm thinking that was a good shot, my ball went further
than my dad's.
He said luck, beginner's luck.
Ready for my second shot smack, thunk . . .
. . . topped it only went three feet.
My dad ready for his second shot smack, thunk right into a goose, walking
across the fairway, the goose squealed like a pig
"Birdie" I shouted.
After the game, we walked to the truck, just me and Gooseman

Centreville Junior High School

The Linebacker Blitz

Braun Crumpton

First, secure a stance with
back arched and knee bent,
arms cocked like pistol hammers,
and sights fixed on the backfield.
Hear the cadence:
down,
blue sixty-nine,
set
. . . waiting for motion.
The charge begins.
A split second before the snap,
timer in the heart tells
the legs when to churn.
As the center lifts the ball,
and the line raises brow,
you're at full speed.
By now, it's too late
for the guard, slow
from his stance.
With face mask cross hairs
on the hand off point,
prepare for collision.
Teeth clenched and
eyes afire,
imagine making the hit
a few feet behind the
approaching fullback.
As your helmet meets
the jersey numbers,
explode through his momentum.
Curl the hips,
driving,

until you feel
the earth.

St. Joseph High School

Metamorphosis of a Swimmer

Aubree Benner

I stand before the fiberglass block
Laying my hands upon it,
Hunching my back like a Halloween cat,
Letting each muscle stretch.
I snap my arms like rubber bands;
Right, left, right, left.
Then I swing them around like windmills
On a gusty day.
I jump up, shaking every limb on my body,
As I gaze down that turquoise path.
I step up once
I step up a second time,
Looking to my
left   right
   and
—Enemies
What's their time?
What's their rank?
It really doesn't matter now it's just
Me and the wake.
A bomb of adrenaline explodes in my chest.
I hate the feeling of pressure.
From a vertical position my body
Gradually comes down.
My hands grab the edge as if it is my only
Support from falling off.
The piercing sound echoes through the air
I spring forward,
The once flat blue surface,
Is now a sea of foam.
I'm transformed into a waterproof butterfly,
Wings made of muscle and flesh.
I fly like I've never flown.
Free from the cocoon I tried to break through

So many times
Before

St. Joseph High School

Brown Fence Ballpark

Jeremy Shermak

With baseball in hand and mind,
stand with me near the flower bed,
there is first,
just beyond the green clothesline

and on second sits a rock
near the thin shed
ignoring the exploding green trees from above

stumble into third
but don't trip on the candy cane slide
home is beneath our feet
balded by the glory of accomplishment

If you can hit it to Baldwin,
Tim told me,
you are the next Babe Ruth
and I smiled
sighed at the smell of trees that interrupted foul balls
and swung my arms like hammers,
the ball splashed through reflecting leaves
and hit off the brown fence

imagination spurs experience and
Lou Gehrig played between our brown fence
the Babe drank the finest whiskey in our shed,
and Joltin' Joe chalked his hits on the garage floor
following the ninth frame

trading strategies with the crickets,
the simplicity of trading cards and eight-year-oldism
caused me to chip paint off the garage

wait for sunrise
and attempt to wake the mighty Casey.

St. Joseph High School

It Came From Right Field . . . And It Was Naked

Doug Mains

It was a warm, sunny summer morning, a morning I will remember my entire life. It started like any other morning, but no, it definitely wasn't any other morning.

I woke up early, since I can never sleep when I'm excited, like on Christmas or Easter. I ate breakfast, probably Lucky Charms. Then my parents woke up, ate breakfast. Yeah, what ever. Then we hopped in the car, and drove to Detroit.

Well, we were going to Detroit to see the Tigers play. Hey, it was 1992 they were kinda good that year. I don't know why we went. I guess just to do something different. So, we drove there. Yeah, pretty normal so far. All right, but wait.

I was excited about the game. Seeing all the players I had watched on TV. Yeah, I know what you're thinking. An average kid taking part in "America's Pastime," but, don't put the story down yet. It gets better.

We found our seats, and watched the players stretch and warm-up. That's when it happened. By it I mean a fate which changed my day, my life, and certainly my feelings about Cecil Fielder.

I noticed a large group of kids hovering around one spot. Then I realized they were waiting for autographs from Cecil Fielder. Like I said it was 1992, he was good back then. So, I grabbed a pen and got in line. Well, a half an hour went by, and I was next in line. I was so excited. Then, Mr. Fielder said, "That's the last one kids."

"Aagh. But I'm next, just one more please," I pleaded.

"Sorry kid, that's the last one."

Fine. I get it. I never liked that fat tub anyway.

Well, then the game went as usual, ate popcorn, hot dogs, drank pop, pretty basic stuff. Then in the 5th inning I really had to go. I mean *really, really* had to go. So my dad took me to the bathrooms, of course, there was a line a mile long. So we waited, and waited, and waited. About half an hour later we came back. My mom said while we were waiting a home run ball came right where we were sitting. And the guy in front of us, reached up and caught it. Bare-handed, c'mon barehanded? I think he broke his hand. I think he broke his hand. I hope he broke his hand. That could've been my ball.

Well, after that the game went pretty smooth. That is until the 8th inning. Think it's amazing how one inning can change a game? Well what if one game changes a life?

A man jumped out of the right field bleachers. Now, the right field bleachers are in direct sun, so it was hot. So I guess he wanted to cool off, so he took off his clothes. I also guess he wanted to take a walk. So he did. On the field. Right into right field. Well, the right fielder sure didn't run too fast to get away from him. And, the guy next to me sure couldn't put the binoculars down that fast, either. Well, he ran around for five minutes, then five policemen "escorted" him off the field. Well, that was my trip, the trip that changed my life, needless to say I haven't gone to a Tigers' game since, and I've never felt the same about baseball since. I now know that going to the ballpark isn't always happy and exciting, sometimes nudists jump out of the stands and fat guys won't sign autographs for you. I really hate the Tigers.

Gull Lake Middle School

The Box

Ilea Swinehart

We sit mindless
Watching
Staring
Not blinking
I wonder if I should get up
For another glass of warm pop
My mother says
"Why don't you go outside?"
My brother responds
Without taking his eyes off the box
On the other end of the room
"Because"
"It is nice out," she persists
"We are busy"
I tell her
And again we sit
Staring at the screen
Like zombies
Only pausing
to search for the remote

Centreville Junior High School

My First Flight

Nathan R. Johnson

When I was young I dreamed of flying. I tried to imagine what it was like to fly like a bird. To soar high up in the sky with the clouds. In fourth grade my dream became a reality.

In fourth grade I had a teacher called Mr. Chatman. Mr. Chatman is the kind of person that it seems impossible to dislike. Every year he does a unit on flight. He teaches us how an airplane flies, and things like that. Anyone who can pass the test at the end would get to fly in an airplane. I passed.

I felt very anxious as my mom drove me to the Allegan County Airport. Mr. Chatman's friend was the pilot. The pilot was a very nice person. He showed me all about his plane. The pilot offered to let me sit in the front, but I didn't. As we left the runway my stomach felt queasy. The next thing I remember is flying high above the ground.

Looking down at the ground at first all I could see was a lot of trees. I figured that must be the Allegan Forest. I also noticed water everywhere. I never realized there were so many lakes in the area. The swimming pools were very strange looking. They had a funny blue color. I don't remember seeing any people except for my parents. You could really see a lot from up high.

It wasn't long before the pilot told me we had to land. Someday I hope to go flying again. This was an experience I'll never forget.

Fennville Middle School

Separating Seeds and Guts

Maureen McCarty

Drazily the van moves on
the rhythmic motor makes us sleepy
Everything on Sunday afternoon makes us sleepy
Family piled into the warm van
feelings mixed between, fun time and waste of time
We head through the country and
roll down the window for the cool air
of fermenting grapes

We pull onto the rough side road
and feel rocky ground beneath the tires
Slowly we park, the side door crashes open
we spill out like jacks
Running row to row
pumpkin to pumpkin
through the orderly patch
To spot the best potential jack-o-lantern
Finding our orange treasure
Lifting it by the stem
Be careful,
that's not the way we carry a pumpkin
cradling it in our arms

We pile back into the van
this time with six more passengers
Riding home with the melting butter sun
the lull of the motor not as exhausting now

We buzz through the glowing kitchen
planning the design and cutting
performing surgery on this orange head
Sitting around the newspaper island
separating guts and seeds
Cleaning the room of the pumpkin innards and riotous laughter

leaving sickening smells and content feelings
We place the faces to stare back in at us from the porch
we give them life with candles
Sitting inside in the dark, looking out
arguing whose is the best
As the lights in all twelve of us slowly burn out

St. Joseph High School

How I Got My Broken Arm

Tyler Boonstra

I was in third grade, not exactly my brightest age. I still remember how I got my cast for my broken arm. It happened right after all the cold lunch students were excused to go outside to the playground. I was still hungry and all I could think about was recess so I took the chips my mom had packed me and headed outside into the warm sunlight of spring. As I walked outside, I munched on chips. Seeing none of my friends were outside yet, I headed toward the old metal swing. You could tell the swing was old by looking at the faded red paint on the bars. I walked up to the swing and took a seat. I started pumping so I could go as high as the swing could go. Every time the swing would go forward I let go of the chain, grabbed a chip, put it in my mouth before the swing would go back. I would always keep a hand on a metal chain so I would not go flying forward. I kept pumping going faster and higher. I was going faster than I thought. I grabbed for another chip. I put the chip in my mouth . I went to grab the chain and didn't make it in time. I flew back. My hand ripped from the chain and I was fully airborne. I was only in air for seconds not knowing what happened. Then landing on my back, I found my left arm beneath me. Tears came to my eyes, and I didn't cry. A student came up to me and asked if I was OK, and I said everything was fine.

The next day x-rays showed that my arm was broken and a cast was put on. The cast was dark blue and later I had everyone in my class sign it. Six weeks after I got my cast, the Doctor took it off. I was scared of swings for a long time. The lesson that I learned was never swing while eating chips.

Fennville Middle School

A Structure of the Heart

Mary Ellen Hund

It was late and the still air was stagnant with the lingering smell of pencil shavings, disinfectant, and wet clothing. A spider crawled its way toward a future home amid the packed box of dog-eared books as if eager to explore the dark recesses for knowledge. I wondered if it could possibly know the stories of this place, loved by many and maligned by some until later in their lives when they realized what it has meant to them. Each concave granite step worn down over the ages; each slate board dulled by years of algebraic equations and spelling words; and each old clock ticking away in its oak frame would have interesting stories to tell if the objects could speak. If only they could relate the memories. . . .

Joe entered the new red brick building in 1916 eager to learn. He admired the stone murals, statues, and the paintings of George Washington and famous artists as they hung down by chains from the oak molding. His lessons consisted of geometry, memorization of literary works, elocution, and Latin. Soon talk would be of war, but for now, he was happy to enjoy the surroundings and the new school as he gazed down North Broadway at some automobiles and work weary horses.

Joyce looked down excitedly at her new saddle shoes and swung her skirt as she walked up the granite stairs to her new classes. Things had not changed much since her father, Joe, went to school here. She wondered if the wooden oak desks with the ink wells were the same ones her father had sat in. She could see initials scratched in the wood and contemplated who the owner might be. The spring and fall seasons were still warm in this building, but the buzz of learning continued. Students talked of war in history classes and some of the boys were eager to sign up to see the world and serve their country with pride. Joyce was looking forward to the J-Hop which would be held in the East Gym with its elevated running track and its creaky wooden floors.

Linda looked down at her lined paper and dreamily wrote "I love the Beatles" hoping the teacher, in her crisp white blouse and stark suit, wouldn't notice. Chrome and plastic furniture which adorned the classroom were in obvious contrast with the old oak molding, wooden floors, and steamy radiators. She glanced up and then gazed toward Mary Beth who, with a frown on her face, was memorizing her vocabulary words. Mary Beth had just bought a snappy new outfit—polished white tennies, plaid kilt, and a mohair sweater. Linda shifted her gaze out of the window to North Broadway where she noticed a sharp, 1967 blue Mustang turning the corner near the Standard Station. Dreams. Oh well, tonight she needed too practice her clarinet in the band room which was added on to the brick building not to many years ago, just after her cousin Joyce graduated.

"Ugly," Jenny thought, "Why don't they get rid of this old brick school. The hallways were too narrow, the East Gym always smells of yesterday's cafeteria special, and it's hot in here! Besides, I don't see why we have to turn this old school into a Junior High. We always get the cast-offs. My Grandpa Joe went here so I know it's old!" She doodled "Make Love Not War!" all over her new Rolling Stone folder as she looked down North Broadway toward the new National Bank of Hastings.

"Well, it's about time," said Josh as he checked out the lowered ceilings and the new carpeting of the old section. His dad had told him the architect said the old brick building was worth saving. Even with a "spiffy" new media center, multi-purpose room, and new seventh grade section, the character of the old school was still there. He remembered what Great-Grandpa Joe had said about going to school here, and he thought about that as he shoved his *Skills for Adolescence* workbook into his backpack and threw on his Red Wings jacket.

I watched the spider weave its magic around a worn *Warriner's English Grammar and Composition*. As I closed the door of the old oak closet, I thought about Joe, Joyce, Linda, Jenny and Josh along with so many others—all harboring memories of this wonderful place. Soon, I too, would take my memories and leave for a new segment of my life after so many years of walking up the granite stairs of the old brick school. The echoes of voices of students pleading about lost homework, contemplating a difficult question, crying over a lost boy/girlfriend, and cheering at a sporting event traveled with me. The sounds of the school . . . the bells, morning announcements, footfalls and tapping, creaky floors, and shrieking voices all walked me to the door. I took one last look down North Broadway where the trees were waving in the breeze and the windows of the old, abandoned City Hall seemed to gaze at me. I wanted to tell it not to fear destruction for I knew that structures of the heart would never die.

Tiny-Tot-Tumbling Class

Sally Renfro

My mommy walks sexy.
She taught me how to
shake my toosh.
(a discouraging frown)
Miss Sally, Madison, she um,
she said the s, x, word.
—Don't be such a
tattle tale Taylor.—
A tiny germ covered index finger
poke, poke, poking my hip.
—What Olivia?—(a little too harshly)
Clasped hands
wedged as a barricade
between her knocking knees,
urgency in her
wide brown eyes,
I have to go to the bafroom.
Uria contentedly talks to himself in a distant corner,
Katelynn
stubs her pinkie toe again;
she's certain she needs stitches,
or at least
a Rugrats Band-aid.
I wanna go home to
my mommy!
—Just five more minutes Austin,
Miss Sally wants her mommy too.—

St. Joseph High School

Rockyette

Megan Hufnagle

She has small ears Not very big at all.
Spiky hair is quite out of style but she seems to be out of style any ways.
Little eyes that are red as fire when she's horridly mad.
Big nose that she uses to smell China with.
Little mouth to keep skinny with.
She's a girl that thinks she's a boy.
She wears her snake necklace that her boyfriend gave her everyday.
Lives in a tent that has a tent in it that she keeps her food in.
She works in a Rock and Roll band.
Her boyfriend is a Maniac and everybody calls him Igor.
She wears bellybutton showing Spaghetti straps.
She wears Tie-dye bellbottoms.
Big soul tennis shoes.
Spiral around her arm.
Earrings all the way up her ear.
Her nose is pierced.
Her eyebrow is pierced.
Last Her lip is pierced.

Howe Elementary

The Teacher and the Student

Jim Sadler

Her hair was a salon special, orange, sixty dollars easy.
She wore a long dress, black, spaghetti shoulder straps.
Her hips, like crossbars, stretched her dress into corners,
And her permanent pelvic thrust was aimed at all
Who stood in front of her.
Her thin mouth, pursed from years of using imperative sentences,
Creased her face, in perfect harmony with her new age image.
In her hand she held a coffee cup, pink, for gender's sake,
And sipped the beans' energy for her epiphanies.
She was my teacher, no role model, but a model anyhow.
She said her life was ordered according to timed writes,
Thesis statements, and three-part papers.
She said treat me like you would a queen,
And fete me every day.
Once she told the class she was a witch,
With three nipples instead of two,
And would have been hung at Salem,
For such an anomaly.
She wanted her students, like satellites, to orbit her womb,
As she sucked them all inside of her,
Prepping them there for a still birth.
As for me, already alive and growing, I resisted entry and left for other worlds.

Elders

Mary G. DeYoung

My mother's sisters greet her warmly
Then they sit in the room of their youth,
Three elderly sisters
Shrunken by age and illness
To forms barely recognizable
Even to each other.
My sister and I observe—
Not quite part of their sisterhood.

Left fatherless at an early age
They now remember their sainted mother.
Reinventing her warm nature
And giving ways,
They search in each other to find her image
And fail.

The youngest sister at 83,
Sits in her wheelchair
Watching birdlike.
She hides secrets behind benign demeanor.
Usually quick with a joke,
She sets aside the humorous
For much more serious matters.
At lunch she hints at her tenuous tomorrow—
"I was afraid we wouldn't have the chance
        to see each other."

The middle sister, almost 85,
Hunched around porous bones,
Peers ahead of her body.
She's quick of tongue, this one,
Equally ready to dismiss as to praise.
She gazes out the window at the gardens
Once beautiful, now gone wild,

That were her domain in years past.
She fills us in on recent visitors.
"Uncle Pete's girls were here Tuesday,"
She says
(The youngest of these girls is 93).

Our mother at 88 has a renewed view of the world
Since her cataract surgery.
Her greatest failing is her memory,
Lost, but she doesn't remember how long ago.
Lost, too, is her hearing aid,
God knows where.
For the third time this afternoon
She asks if the youngest can sleep well.
The answer is again affirmative.
Later as the middle sister leaves the room
To fix tea,
Mother says, to no one in particular,
"She doesn't look like my sister anymore."

The afternoon draws to a close
In this grand old home.
With huge oriental rug and the rich mahogany furniture—
the same as when I was ten
Except for the hospital bed, wheelchair, and oxygen tank.
These old women
Spin out long silences filled with memory.
My sister and I struggle to fill the silence
And wonder why we try.
We came expecting their wisdom;
Instead we witness their frailty.
We stand to say our good-byes,
And retreat to our own lives,
Refusing to see ourselves in these women,
Relieved to have done our duty,
Determined to age with grace.

Constantine

Joyce N. Hunter

freshly cut hay particles tickle the inside of my nose
as tractors rumble down dirt roads, leaving wrinkles in the road.
Dogs casually trot down unmarked roads and stop to drink in the creek
where young kids play, hoping not to get sucked in by the leeches.
Corn tassels lay idle on mounds of dirt, as stalks are raped through August
it's good money kids say,
as they pee among dirt and trees, fervidly waiting for it to be over.

In town, decrepit buildings stand beaten
wind and rain
as the mighty St. Joe careens through town, dividing the corn from the buildings.

Harvey House Hotel
Gambles
Jinny's Boutique
Nip and Sip
Village Inn
Town Fryer

these are symbols, along with the old man who walked funny down the street
    (rumor
had it he was hit by a car)
the hotel (which really isn't, but a restaurant)
the hardware store (which really isn't, but an abandoned building)
the beauty shop (which really is, for those over sixty)
the bar (whose owner died of cancer)
the restaurants (one for those who cannot bear to walk outside of town, the other
    for
those who dare to test the city limits).

Village Pizza Plus—the pizza place (which really was)

a storefront of decay, like all the rest

peeling paint that walks down the sidewalks and sticks to windows
crumbling mortar that struggles to hang on, yet falls when the spring thaw comes
Inside
electric lights
gleaming booths
glowing ovens
blaring jukeboxes
ringing phones
dancing waitresses
Life.

I come here to unwind, to experience the life of a teenager
as friendly voices surround me.
I come back week after week for my sanity
burping contests
first kisses
cheesy pizzas
milkshakes
the best garlic toast in town.

These are my symbols
life struggling to survive among crumbling ashes
as my body grows, so does my mind.

I have to get out
get out of this geriatric prison.

Hay and corn aren't "quaint" anymore
tractors don't move fast enough
they are chains
old people go with buildings
they aren't "sophisticated" anymore
they are steel bars.

I have to get out
get out of this geriatric prison.

"I hate this town"
"How gross"

"I can't wait to get out of this hellhole"

get out before you become one of those girls
who marries a local boy who just happens
to be a farmer or mechanic
have four kids before age twenty-five
spend days wiping snotty noses
and watching kids swim in the muddy river among fish nobody eats.

Get out because you deserve so much better than this
break the chains, saw the steel bars
don't get sucked into the cycle
escape.

first college degree
first love
first marriage
first job
first pet
first home
first heartache
first death
first craving for something more that cannot be bought.

what is it?

I find myself in a cornfield where tassels haven't been picked yet
it's too early
knee high by the fourth of July
remember?
there is something gregarious about tractors
serenity now.

I find myself at Village Pizza Plus, craving garlic bread and cheesy pizza
it's no longer there
the sanity of my youth turned into a video store
memories hidden forever under the science fiction and drama sections,
waiting to be checked out by someone else.

why am I here?

the chains were broken and bars were stripped down,
and yet I return to the prison
am I a glutton for punishment.

where are the prison guards?
    in the fields?
        on the tractors?
            on the street corner?
                in the video store?

Uptown Girl

Sheri L. Willems

A few years ago, Kim, a classmate from Vicksburg, referred to me as an "uptown girl" because of the way I dressed for class that night. The occasion didn't merit anything special—a graduate class at Western Michigan University. On that particular night, I wore pastel pink slacks, with a pastel pink and mint green sleeveless top, low heels, and a simple gold earring and necklace set . . . fakes. One of my teaching outfits. No time to change. My schedule was tight.

Before driving the hour and fifteen minutes to Kalamazoo for my six o'clock class, I rustled up dinner . . . fried chicken, fresh sweetcorn, mashed potatoes and gravy, hot buttered biscuits, and a tossed salad topped with vine ripened cherry tomatoes. The kids wouldn't starve, and I knew they were safe in our rural house which even friends had trouble finding the first few times.

Kim's comment startled me because I'd wrestled with the idea of an easier, more glamorous city life, where public schools spring up within a block or two of home, colleges are just around the corner, grocery stores open early across the street, and public transportation makes it easy to live without a car.

But, now, after visiting friends in Toronto, my cousin Ruthie in Chicago, Anna Sirhan in San Francisco, my cousin, James, in Portland, and a myriad of other city dwellers, I realize my real sense of place is rural. I'm a country girl born and bred. I'd miss the night sounds of crickets, tree frogs, bullfrogs by the ponds and swamps, and the thousands of buzzing insects that sing me to sleep every night.

I'd miss my black and white striped furry friend that sneaks into the garage to eat the cat food, once even brushing against my legs, as I stood outside after dusk listening to the night sounds. I thought it was the cat until the white stripe glistened in the moonlight. Luckily, my fuzzy friend didn't spray!

How could I live without picking the blueberries that stain my fingers but make succulent snacks; or climbing over the fence to follow the edge of the corn rows, plucking juicy wild black raspberries from their prickly bushes whose thorns leave red welts on my hands?

I'd even miss the pungent smell of manure on the freshly turned field near the house, and the bellowing of Mr. Peterson's cows, a half mile away. They set up a real racket when he's late for milking.

What would the rabbits, squirrels, deer, opossums, raccoons, birds, and pesky woodchucks do without my garden as part of their daily diet?

How could I survive without the soft hoot of the wise old owl that lives in the sassafras tree outside my study window, soothing me with his sound, which even echoes down the chimney sometimes on chilly October nights.

Sometimes I might look like an uptown girl, but I don't think about living in the city anymore. In my heart, I'll always be rural, a country gal, who knows how to bake bread from scratch, make fluffy dumplings and fresh fruit pies, can peaches, plant spices, grow pumpkins . . . and even dig up the septic tank when it needs to be pumped!

Summer Memories

Dave Hocker

I have memories of my yard. When we first moved to this house, it seemed as big as Montana, especially compared with my minute yard in town, where I had lived for as long as I could remember. So at the age of seven, this became my first yard. I loved it, and have for the seven years that I've lived here.

The house rests on a large hill. In winter, trying to drive up it is like trying to climb Mt. Everest. In the front side yard, is a partially wooded area we call the "bunny trails" due to a vast population of rabbits that live there. We used to play Cowboys and Indians there, and if you were brave enough you could walk through the twisting trails at night. I used to see how close I could get to a rabbit before it would bolt away like a dog running from a bath. The driveway goes up the hill, then wraps around the back of the house and levels out. From the house back, the property is flat.

The back, which is mainly wide open, is about 100 yards. In the middle are four trees, in the shape of a rectangle. They form two perfect soccer goals or end zones, for a quick game with my brother, or practice. Woods on all sides enclose the rest of the back yard. A few trails run through them. This part of the property is great for "capture the flag" and other late night games with friends.

At the back edge of the property is a pole barn built by my dad. He uses the downstairs as his shop, where he fixes old cars, and the upstairs is storage. A gravel lane winds around the side of the property, connecting the barn and the driveway. Mulberry trees are scattered randomly about the yard. The small berries provide a sticky, sweet snack, or "face paint." I always try to grab some off a tree while I buzz past on the riding lawn mower. So much to do, so many sweaty, barefooted summer days spent there. Even the driveway is home to many basketball and roller hockey games.

We used to have a bag swing burlap bag stuffed with cloth hanging from a large oak tree in the side yard. It was exhilarating to swing on until my golden retriever thought that chewing it up would be fun. I will always remember this wonderful yard, will always look back at the grass stains and dandelions. When I remember the days with watermelon juice, sticky as tape, dripping down my chin, as I spit the seeds in the freshly cut grass, I will smile.

Gull Lake Middle School

Ode to My Place

Kathryn Reber

To the pasture that feeds my horses
Fresh grass when they are hungry,
Full of luscious yellow dandelions,
That reflect the bright morning sun.
And the tree that fell like a wounded soldier
During that storm last fall.

To the dusty sand that Star and Willie roll in
When they have an itch they can't scratch.
And to the electric fence
That bit me like a rabid dog
When I got too close.

To the leafy green vines
that scratch me when I ride under them,
And to my horses tall and elegant,
two watchmen protecting my treasure.

Centreville Junior High School

Allegan County Fair

Sarah Hazen

One of the best memories I have is going to the fair. When I was younger my parents and I always went to the Allegan County Fair. We would look around at all the animals and watch people show off all the work they went through to get their animals ready.

When we got around to the goat barn I wanted to stay long to look at the baby goats and every time I would ask if we could get one and every time the answer was no. I sat down and started to pout, but when my dad mentioned the rides, I got up and started off without them. I asked if I could go on the Ring of Fire, but my mom said I don't think so. I decided to go on the space ship ride and then go somewhere else. After the ride we went to go get a couple of elephant ears and go home.

I now enter my animals and myself into the fair. The goats I wanted I have and a rabbit too. Each year I get a buck, a male goat to sell. I feed him all summer long and walk him on a leash. When it comes time to bring him to the fair, I load him, a few other goats and the rabbit into the car and go.

When I first get to the fair I take the male and get him weighed; he must weigh at least 30 pounds to stay and get sold. I show them on certain days and I get ribbons for them, sometimes blue and sometimes red. The blue stands for first and the red for second. When I was younger I always liked it when the judge would go out there and hand someone a blue ribbon and see that person's face light up like a beam. Now the crowd can see my face light up.

On Wednesday, the last week of the fair I sell the buck at the auction and go and shake the hands of the buyer and give him a picture of the goat and I. On that Saturday they pick him up and take him to the slaughterhouse. Sometimes I get to see him go and sometimes I don't. That same day I go to the office and pick up my money for the ribbons I earned. The amount I get depends upon how many I get, what color the ribbons are, and what I got the ribbon for. Later they will send me the rest of the money for the goat. On the following day I bring the rest of the animals home and rest. Each year I do this and have such a good time I look forward to the next year.

Wayland Middle School

Dear Love,

Alison Strasser

I waited
for 30 cold minutes
    Heart stopping
with every flash
of headlights
    passing.
And when I heard
your car approach
And smelled your
    clove and cigar scent
my relief
    overwhelmed
my sudden urge
    To scream
    Or cry
And I forced a smile through
    My unnoticed frustration
As you told the story
    Of outrunning a cop,
    Taking back roads
I drifted away
    Remembering
How you sent me
    Sweet folded napkin messages
        On busy days
encouraged my smile
    And happiness
even when I was crying
How you held my hand,
called me Babe
    And I didn't mind
How we sat outside
    For hours

In the cold, late winter night
    Until we couldn't
put sentences
    together anymore
And that's why
    I waited

St. Joseph High School

How to Ease Your Mind

Josh Butzbaugh

You need to grab some fresh blueberries
Bigger the better
Fill the blender with berries along with some milk and ice cream
make your mixture thick, then pour it in a mug
walk on to the end of the pier
sit down on the edge
as the sun touches the horizon, relax
don't let any thought corrupt you
once the night greets you, smile back
touch your feet to the water
drop your clothes, dive in
float on your back
let the moon inspire your dreams
chat with God
understand no one can bring you down
climb out, sit still
the breeze will wash away the past
dry your outsides

St. Joseph High School

Outlined by Rain

Maureen McCarty

Staring at the window
more than looking out
it's definitely fall in South Haven
a yellow fall not
a beautiful autumn
outlined by rain

I write
my finger the chalk
your window my blackboard
on the steamy glass
you always said it would come true
if you erased it
I lie down
tucked up
my boots against the door
burying my head
in the wool sweater
you gave me last Christmas
wet and rough it smells
like youth fair barns
the CD spins

Remembering when you sang
my brown-eyed girl
replaced with blue
for me
I bat heavy lids over
my dark blues
to sprinkle tears on
my hot checks
I wish you'd turn the heater down
but don't ask

I hear you just
slightly softer
than the music
Is she asleep
I shut my eyes
and try
to breathe
deep
and
rhythmically

St. Joseph High School

My Town, Not Yours

Stephanie Ann Miller

So, I went to the beach today
in my town, not yours
I took him with me, and we made discoveries
I saw a dog, and of course I have seen that before
but today, that dog, whose name started with an "M,"
he dug a hole, and stuck a stick in
Now, I know this has happened before, and I even know it is a
        frequent occurrence
But I had never seen it before today, not ever
I am half way to many pre-middle ages, and I have never seen That
I have seen my significant things, like once, I saw a teeny, tiny cat
His mother was not so swift, and she let him drop right out of her
        womb, and on to the ground
Where a bee started to eat his small, curled ear.
Being a compassionate girl, my best friend and I saved him, by
        doing the most bestest thing we could
We told her mom.
So as you see, I have seen things more significant than dogs digging
        holes
But, now that I have seen that, I have started to fill in some space
Space where something was void
Space that was skipped over, and ignored
When it should have been paid attention to.
And that dog, he wasn't even digging a good hole, the sand kept
        falling in every time he dug it out, none-the-less, I saw it.
Then he and I found rocks, not that they were hard to find
He picked the biggest ones, and was so immensely proud of
        himself that I carried every one up from the shore line
And I kept them, and I will always keep them
I found rocks too.
One has a hole right through it . . . all the way through
What could do that to a rock, what penetrates a rock?
Whatever it is, it must be special, you know?

The next rock I found has a dark, coffee color running
    around it, in a perfect outline.
Absolutely perfect, not outside the lines at all
And inside the lines is a smooth caramel oval
It almost looks like it will be soft when you touch it, but it isn't
It could withstand anything, even whatever it was that pushed
    through the other rock.
And I found one more rock worth keeping, it's not any shape
Except its the same shape as a penny that I put on the
    railroad tracks when I was twelve
I would go the next day and search and search for my penny
Which was worthless to everyone but me, not even worth one cent
But it was so shiny and smooth, and not any shape whatsoever.
I liked it, and it was mine.
So, before the sun touched the water, we two left
And I felt better and he was sleepy
And I sang the radio song all the way home
And after I had cried a little bit, it was good, and I knew where I
    was again.

Grande Mere Inn

Dan Holt

Imagine we're sitting in this restaurant, and we're watching this woman as if she were a character in a movie. We're doing this partly because there are very few surprises in our own lives and partly because it's fun to make our own movies. The first scene, the one before we even get inside, shows this quaint restaurant, on this bluff, overlooking sand dunes and a very large body of water. That large body of water is Lake Michigan. The light is sort of orange because the sun is setting over the dunes and the water. The camera eye then moves inside and focuses on a woman (her name is Sue) sitting by herself at a table in the corner. You and I are background characters: a middle aged man and his wife out for a quiet dinner, talking about their children and mortgage payments.

Sue has been sitting in the Grande Mere Inn for almost 30 minutes, basking in a very good Friday feeling. The sun, setting over the dunes and the lake, casts a soft golden light over the small restaurant. The place is packed with talking and laughter, and Sue is enjoying the view and enjoying being seated in this room filled with so many happy people. After all, she is sitting at her favorite table: the one in the corner, next to the stone fireplace, the one with the view of the dunes and the lake beyond. It is still early; the night is going to be as beautiful as the sunset.

Then the story really starts because there is another character (his name is Tim) to reckon with, someone who Sue apparently knows well and maybe has been waiting for. She spots Tim, who is taking off his overcoat, preparing to hang it up on the coat rack on the wall, next to a sign that says the management is not responsible for the coats if someone walks off with them. She catches his eye and he waves, but he doesn't smile. We think to ourselves that something must be wrong in paradise if Tim doesn't smile at Sue. This is sort of like foreshadowing, but we don't take it all that seriously. There's going to have to be more evidence before we get nervous for Sue. Just once, we think, it would be nice if nothing bad happened to the main character of our story; after all, we're already beginning to like Sue.

Tim must have had a tough time getting out of the city, Sue thinks to herself. She left a few hours before, but the traffic was heavy even then. She went on ahead to get the room. Besides, it wouldn't look good for them to be seen leaving together. Sue and Tim had been able to keep their affair secret, but it had not been easy. Tim, she thinks, must have been tied up at the office. She decides to give him a warm smile as he, looking preoccupied and entirely too serious for a glorious Friday night, approaches the table.

The reason we know what Sue is thinking is she has a very expressive face: her thoughts are relayed to us through her eyes, the way she holds her mouth, the tilt of her head. Because we often go to the movies, we are good at deciphering these facial gestures. We look at each other and smile when we figure out what Sue is thinking. She is 40 and fadingly pretty, her features softer now that she has achieved maturity. Her hair is light brown and done in short curls. Her eyes, large and very brown, dominate her face. Her thin lips, cut sharply in the corners, are not often smiling as broadly and easily as they are tonight. She is wearing her best dress, the red dress that Tim, her boss and lover, gave her.

"What's wrong?" she asks.

Tim sits across from her and takes her hand, cupping it between his hands. "Just a tough day," he says, glancing at her and smiling weakly. His blazer is unbuttoned, and he has loosened his tie. He looks tired to Sue.

"Tim, you look beat. Right after dinner, we'll go to the motel. OK?"

Sue has been sneaking off with Tim for almost a year, sometimes weeknights at her place (she lives alone) or occasionally a weekend out of town when Tim's wife is away on buying trips for a large chain store. Sue and Tim work together, but she is proud of the way they are able to keep their personal lives out of the work place. That is something they agreed on from the outset: they would be all business at business; there would be no indication of their private lives at work, no little glances, caresses, or notes, not at work. They had both worked too hard to get to where they were to blow it all with an office romance.

Sue, you and I agree, has given up a great deal for her career. She has never been married, even though she had chances. She was too busy for a husband and family. She became known as an up-and-comer, one of those likely to take up residency in one of the offices upstairs. It took longer than she expected, but it happened. After 17 years with the firm, Sue was named the first female vice-president in the company's history. That's when she began working with Tim, who was younger than she but talented. He was the CEO's right-hand man and well-connected. Tim had married into the controlling interest of the company, a marriage he said of convenience. This is all stuff that we get through looks, body language, and genre. I mean, this is how it is with up-and-comers. This is not such an unusual story after all.

Still the movie is in its introduction stage. We're just getting used to the air conditioning and the dark, munching quietly on salad, feeling pretty good about the characters. But we know something bad is going to happen. After all, this would be a pretty boring story if Sue and Tim just ate their dinner and went to the motel and made love and then went back to Chicago. I mean, it happens every day, but who would spend seven bucks to see this in a movie, unless, of course, the love scene was particularly graphic.

"Something's wrong," says Sue. "What is it?"

Tim doesn't answer right away. He still seems preoccupied. He's staring out across the parking lot, into the darkness, picking at his tossed salad with house dressing.

"Tim, you can tell me. What's the matter?"

He looks at her really for the first time that evening. "She knows."

We knew that would happen. The wife would have to find out sooner or later. Sue also knew this would happen and was ready. She almost smiled; we caught that very fleeting upturn of the lips. Women can do that but men aren't subtle enough; they show too much teeth.

"I see," Sue says as she dips a small piece of crab into butter sauce. She studies the morsel for a moment and then delicately places the crab into her mouth, chewing the way her mother said she should chew. She then dabs the sharp corners of her mouth with her napkin, returning the white linen to her lap when she's done.

"Well, what should we do now?" She already knows what she wants done, what she had dreamed; but she wants Tim to come to it himself, to say, "Why, honey, I'll just divorce her and then we can be together. I'm glad it's out in the open."

But he doesn't say that.

There is a pregnant pause here. Somewhere in the background is the sound of the piano from the bar. The performer is playing and singing "Feelings." "Whoa, whoa, whoa, feelings. . . ."

The main course comes. I have the Turf and Surf, and you have that stir fry stuff you like so much. The movie is put on hold until Collette has finished serving. Collette is not an important part of the movie, but she is likely to appear again, if for no other reason than to clean up after the terrible fight that is likely to occur between Sue and Tim, who are just now beginning to become quarrelsome at the table by the stone fireplace with the excellent view of a now completely set sun. We both think this last image is symbolic of their relationship, a nice touch.

"I can't leave her," Tim says without conviction. His words come out almost as a question. And then he says it again; this time with more conviction: "I can't LEAVE her!"

Sue's smile fades now and her eyes begin to tear up; she is biting her lip, and now she turns her head as if she is looking at something in the black parking lot.

Sue is looking into the parking lot as if she is trying to find something she has lost. Again, we think this image is symbolic.

Surprise! We were expecting lots of tears and maybe a loud scene, some shouting, name calling, maybe even a little violence. We are surprised when Sue turns back, her eyes sparkling, a wide-smile, saying, "I know; I guess I always knew."

What she knew is that Tim owes his life to his marriage, his position in the firm, his style. To leave his wife is to leave his job (remember the connections his wife had to the company?) We decide that Tim's father-in-law is the principal stock holder in the company. Divorce would mean dismissal. Tim has worked too damn hard to get where he is to let an office romance ruin it all. We decide that Tim is no Romeo; Tim is a weasel. "Sue!" we want to say out loud. "Sue! You are too good for this guy. Forget him. Listen, we have this friend who's an up-and-comer in advertising. You guys would really hit it off." But of course we don't say anything because this is a movie, and it would be impolite to speak.

"How? How did she find out?"

Tim shrugs his shoulders. "Does it matter?"

"No, I guess not." Sue smiles and says that they shouldn't spoil their last evening together. Poor Sue.

It takes a little bit, but the crisis seems to be over by the time Sue and Tim and you and I are finishing the main course. Tim is scraping the last bit of the white pulp from his baked potato; Sue is regaining her balance. OK, she thinks to herself. I don't have Tim, but I knew he couldn't leave his wife. I'm a grownup. I knew what I was getting into. It's not his fault; it's no one's fault. It just happened, and now it's over.

"I have to go back to the city," Tim says after they order dessert from Collette. "I can't stay."

Sue doesn't say anything in response to this. She figured he would have to go back now, back to his wife. She notices the night is clear and there are stars.

"Sue, I'm sorry." We're surprised that Tim actually looks sorry as he says this. Maybe he isn't such a weasel after all. Maybe he's just a little weak. "I had to come tonight. I couldn't just leave you here waiting, or just call you. But I can't stay." Again, we are astounded by the guy's decency. After all, he drove all that way so he could let her down in person, face to face, lover to lover. "Are you going to be all right?"

"Sure," Sue responds.

Now, Tim has a different look, a look like maybe something he has just eaten is giving him cramps. That look scares us a little. What could be bothering him? we ask ourselves.

Sue also sees the look. "Tim, is there something else?"

"I'm sorry," Tim repeats, "but the old man called me in today and said you would have to go. You'll be given a good reference. He promised me that."

You and I look at each other until the full realization sinks in, and then we see that Tim has pulled himself away from Sue who is sitting dazed. Tim vanishes; Sue is crying loudly enough that Collette has alerted the manager who is coming to comfort her.

We, as audience and eaters, have had our full and get up carefully to leave, not waiting for the credits. But I have to look back just one more time to see if Sue is still sitting there sobbing. She is, but controls herself enough to acknowledge Collette who has brought her the check.

Contributors' Notes

Mary Alaniz was born and raised in rural Branch County, Michigan. She graduated from Union City High School, received a BA degree from Albion College, and has done graduate work in journalism at Ball State University. She has taught English and journalism at Union City High School for twenty years. She is married to Ben Alaniz and has three children, one of whom is also a teacher.

Tom Anderson grew up on a lake in rural West Michigan. He spent his summers swimming, fishing, and obsessing about any all sports. He is a teacher at Edwardsburg Middle School.

Beth Aven is a student at Edwardsburg Middle School and she loves sports. She plays volleyball, basketball, softball, and track. She also like animals and when she grows up, she wants to be an accountant.

Jennifer S. Baggerly was born in Coldwater and spent the majority of her youth in Union City. She received her BA degree from Albion College with majors in English and history. She presently teaches at Colon Junior/Senior High School.

Joe Bartz is, himself, an American male and vacillates, in private, after the fashion of his completely authentic subjects. It is a matter, he says, of investing your leisure thoughtfully and hoping for a modicum of resolution.

Aubree Benner is eighteen years old and will be attending the University of Michigan in the fall to major in Art. She wrote this poem from the experience she had throughout high school on the St. Joseph High School swim team. It basically is expressing the anxiety and thoughts and changes that a complete swimmer may experience.

Sharon Bippus grew up in rural Michigan, but ran away to Chicago after college. She taught school in the inner-city for several years then moved to Southwestern Michigan six years ago. She writes poetry and is finishing a novel. She lives in Three Rivers with her husband and dog and teaches high school in Constantine.

Joseph Andrew Biron II is 11 years old. He has a sister named Barbie and she is 12. He is Native American and a traditional dancer, and he drums with his dad and uncles. When he grows up, his dream is to be a doctor.

Tyler Boonstra lives in the town of Fennville with his mom, dad, and younger brother. He is thirteen and currently is going into the eighth grade. In his spare time, he enjoys reading and playing the computer.

Sherrie Britton has lived in rural Michigan all her life. She is currently working on her MFA in poetry at Western Michigan University and is the Site Coordinator for Rural Voices, Country Schools.

Pamela M. Buchanan lives with her husband and four cats in "The House In the Woods" (in the middle of a beech-maple climax forest) in rural northeastern Kalamazoo County. She has taught in Comstock for twenty-six years, primarily seventh and eighth grade Language Arts at Northeast Middle School. She is a charter fellow of the Third Coast Writing Project, where she discovered what writing really means to her.

Jessie M. Buckingham loves to write children's books and poems. Her hobby is riding her paint horse, Tora. She also enjoys sports.

Adam Burghdoff is a student a Gull Lake Community Schools. He is an athlete and plays sports such as football and baseball.

Rose Burket is a graduate of Eastern Michigan University. Her home is in Benton Harbor until she moves to a retirement home. Her husband was M. E. Burket who was also a graduate of Eastern Michigan University.

Josh Butzbaugh is the person you connected eyes with and saw a last memory, but didn't know where it came from.

Renee Callies. After growing up next to a fruit farm and a lake, Renee Callies keeps the country in her by teaching English at Gull Lake Middle School. She writes in her spare time and has contributed a chapter for a book on teaching grammar, and continues working with Rural Voices, Country Schools and the Third Coast Writing Project.

John Campbell is a 1998 graduate of Lake Michigan Catholic High School and will attend Western Michigan University. His hobbies include reading, photography, and playing pool.

Pen Campbell grew up in the middle of the cornfield sea that is central Illinois. She teaches English at Lake Michigan Catholic High School in St. Joseph and does her best to balance family, teaching, writing, and still work in a little fishing and photography in her spare time. Her poem "Jovon" appeared in *Language Arts Journal of Michigan*, Spring, 1997.

Anna Clark is a senior at St. Joseph High School in St. Joseph, Michigan. She plans to continue her education at a Midwestern University where she will study journalism and English writing. She hopes to pursue a career in professional writing.

Braun Crumpton lives in St. Joseph, Michigan.

A. James DeFields was born on the family farm just outside of Coloma. He was drafted into the Navy during World War II and began a 21-year career in Airborn Electronics. He retired in 1966 and began writing his life story shortly after as something to leave to his children and grandchildren.

Mary G. DeYoung teaches English at Bangor High School. She is a graduate of Hope College and received her Masters from Colorado State University. Her rural heritage is often the subject of her writing.

Melissa Dine lives in St. Joseph, Michigan.

Brittany Lynn Doyle is currently going into the eighth grade at Gull Lake Middle School. She is the youngest of four children. She enjoys playing sports (tennis and basketball are her favorites), playing piano and trombone, hanging around with her awesome friends, and taking care of her four cats (one of which is the mother cat in her story) and two dogs.

Coral J. Fry was born and raised near Sturgis, Michigan, and after high school graduation spent the next eleven years in the Ypsilanti/Detroit area working and attending college. She and her husband decided to come to this area (he is from Grosse Pointe) to live, work and raise a family, which they have done for over twenty years. Her concerns include, but are not limited to, the environment, feminism and equal opportunity for all people.

Elizabeth Haines lives in Richland with her husband, Steve. She is currently working on two mysteries; one set in the 1920's and the other in the 1990's. Both mysteries take place in small towns.

Corey L. Harbaugh teaches English and composition at Gobles High School. Images of Southwest Michigan show up in his fiction, sometimes as heroes, sometimes as villains, but most often as a little of both. He lives with his wife and son in the Kalamazoo area.

Sarah Hazen lives in Hopkins, Michigan.

Patricia Grover Heyn has been a journalist and teacher of English. She is at present writing stories inspired by the village that was her childhood home. She enjoys being a grandmother, writing both prose and poetry, travel with her adult children, and Ireland.

Dave Hocker lives in Augusta, Michigan.

Dan Holt has taught writing at St. Joseph High School for the last twenty-five years. A former Michigan Creative Writing Teacher of the Year, Dan is co-director of the Third Coast Writing Project at Western Michigan University.

Megan Hufnagle is sometimes called Meg. She has a dog named Rudy. Her parents' names are Devanie Stanner and Tony Hufnagle.

Mary Ellen Hund is a teacher of English and drama and is the English Coordinator for Hastings Area Schools. She has also taught journalism and creative writing and has been a speaker in the language arts area at many conferences throughout the state. Two of her passions are writing and photography which she feels helps her "look at life more vividly."

Joyce N. Hunter calls Constantine her home, although she now lives in the "city" of St. Joseph. After graduating from Western Michigan University with a major in English Education in 1995, she began her teaching career at St. Joseph Public Schools. She and her husband, Marc, married in 1996. Through writing poetry she has learned more about her family, her hometown, herself and her *life*.

Peter Hyland was born in Texas and moved to Michigan for seventh grade. He has always enjoyed reading, writing and, of course, marching.

Erik Ivans lives in Niles, Michigan.

Adam J. Johnson is 14 years old and in the 8th grade. He lives on a small farm near Sturgis, Michigan. His interests include 4-H and most sports.

Nathan R. Johnson lives in Pullman, Michigan.

Marie E. Kelley is a retired educator who taught English, Speech and French and served as high school assistant principal, middle school principal, curriculum director and adjunct professor at University of Nebraska and Western Michigan University. She writes a cooking column for the *Allegan County News*, The Gardening Gourmet.

Kristin Kelly lives in St. Joseph, Michigan.

Katherine E. Kendall grew up and went to school in Centreville, Michigan. In high school she enjoyed English and drama. This fall she will attend Eastern Michigan University.

Brad Koch will be attending Belmont University in Nashville, Tennessee, and majoring in music business. He is a music lover and hopes to pursue a career in the popular music industry.

Rebecca Kosick's interests are of nature and art. She loves to write, to paint, and to sail. She is a junior in high school.

Myron J. Kukla is a midwest writer and humorist. His work appears in the *Lakeshore Press* and *Grand Rapids Press*. He was born in Youngstown, Ohio, and graduated from Kent State University with a BS degree in Journalism. He holds a Masters degree in Communications from Western Michigan University. He and his family live in Holland, Michigan, Tulip Capital of the World.

   (Credits: This work was originally published in the *Lakeshore Press* and in the new book (1998) *Confessions of a Baby Boomer: Memories of Things I Haven't Forgotten Yet* by Myron J. Kukla published by Lockport Ent. Ltd.)

E. Blair Laing is nine years old, attends Brown School in St. Joseph, Michigan, and wrote *"A Tree Story"* in third grade. The beautiful farms of Berrien County inspired her to write her story. She spends all her spare time reading and plans to be a writer because she loves books.

Anne L. Lape was a TCWP Fellow in 1996. She is a teacher at the Kazoo School in Kalamazoo.

Grace A. Lucker has lived in Southwest Michigan all of her life. She enjoys boating and Lake Michigan with her husband, Doug, two sons, and three grandchildren. She works in a dental office, has been writing for ten years, and is a member of The Lakeshore Writers.

Doug Mains is an eighth grade student in the Gull Lake School system. He lives with his parents and brother in Augusta. He enjoys playing sports.

Lilly Massa was born in Hershey, Pennsylvania, and grew up in St. Joseph, Michigan. She loves to play soccer and basketball and this year is attending Wake Forest University in Winston-Salem, North Carolina.

Maureen McCarty was born in Seattle, Washington, but has grown up in St. Joseph with her parents, sister, brothers, and cat. She graduated (1998) from St. Joseph High School and will attend the University of Notre Dame in the fall. She loves picking berries, picnicking on the beach, and rereading *The Great Gatsby*.

Jenifer McCauslin is nine years old and in the fifth grade. She has three dogs. Their names are Bowzer, Tyler, and Tracker. She loves to write.

Nikki is a 12 year old seventh grader at Gull Lake Middle School. She enjoys academic challenges, playing the piano, soccer, basketball, and volleyball. Nikki is interested in pursing a career in medicine.

Judy G. McLain teaches *"The Power of Memories"* seminars, encourages journaling and seeking meaning from early experiences that shaped our personality and values. She was raised in cherry country in Elk Rapids, Michigan, lived five years in Southwestern lower Michigan and now resides in rural Oceana County.

Ian McLaren is twelve years old and will be entering eighth grade in the fall. He has one brother and one sister. He goes to Gull Lake Schools.

Ashley B. Mikulyuk is 13 years old and she just recently moved to South Bend, Indiana. She has three pets: one dog, one cat and a green parrot called Pepper. She lives in a nice two-story house with a yellow living room and her room has a blue ceiling!

Stephanie Ann Miller is a twenty year old student at Kalamazoo College. She is the mother to eighteen month old Andrew Mark. She is majoring in English and hopes to develop a career in teaching.

Matt O'Leary is seventeen years old and a member of the class of 2000 at Mattawan High School. He lives on a small rural farm where he enjoys fishing and playing soccer in his spare time.

E. Kevin Owens is going into sixth grade. He lives at home with his mom, dad, sister, Christine and his cat. He likes to play sports and be in the great outdoors.

Scott Peterson is a fourth grade teacher in the Mattawan Schools. He is a graduate of Western Michigan University. He is a co-author of the book *Theme Exploration: A Voyage of Discovery* and has published an essay and lessons to share on teaching grammar in context.

Christina Phillips enjoys working at the St. Joseph Public Library. She grew up on Lake Street. Lake Michigan was her picture window to the world. She is married and has two children.

Amy Prater is ten years old. She will be eleven in April. She will be in fifth grade.

Ian Rastall lives in St. Joseph, Michigan.

Kathryn Reber is an eighth grade student at Centreville Junior High. She has an eleven year old sister named Kelsey, and together they enjoy the many animals they raise on their small farm. She also enjoys reading and participating in 4H.

Sally Renfro lives in St. Joseph, Michigan.

Davey Robison is twelve years old. His favorite sports to play are baseball, golf, and football. His favorite sports cars are a Dodge Viper and a Chevy Corvette. In his spare time he likes to watch television and play Nintendo, and play sports.

Jim Sadler is an older American who was born and raised in Genesee County, farm country. When he left for Kalamazoo, he was sad because he did not understand what he was forsaking. He has worked here for many years as an educator; however, he is also interested in commodities trading, listening and playing blues, fishing, physical fitness, and writing. Keeping his house clean has interfered with his interest in writing; lately, the house has not been as clean.

Jeremy Schnotala grew up in a variety of small towns throughout the upper and lower peninsula of Michigan. He graduated from Calvin College and is working on his Masters degree at Western Michigan University. He currently teaches English, Speech and Drama at Wyoming Park High School in Grand Rapids.

Douglas Andrew Schrock was born in Richmond, Virginia, in 1985. His main interests are the American Civil War, southern history, and fine arts. He wants to be a writer some day.

Whitney Schrubba is an eleven year old and she is in the sixth grade. She loves to sing, dance, and write stories. She dreams of becoming an entertainer when she grows up.

Cheryl Sears lives in Centreville, Michigan.

Jeremy Shermak will be a freshman at Michigan State University in the fall of 1998. He enjoys writing poetry and fiction, but will major in journalism and plans to go into the newspaper field upon graduation. He has worked for a year at the *South Bend Tribune* daily newspaper, in South Bend, Indiana.

Catherine Stasevich is the oldest child in a family of four. She is in 4-H and shows Bantam chickens and harlequin rabbits. She hopes to some day become an artist and professional avian breeder.

Erica L. Stewart is 13 years old and has lived in a small town all her life. She enjoys reading and spending time with her friends.

Alison Strasser is an eighteen year old graduate of St. Joseph High School and attending Western Michigan University in the fall as an occupational therapy major. She began seriously writing when she was fifteen. She also plays cello and works at a summer youth camp teaching archery.

Norma Strong seeks the essence of things and tries to distill her experiences in poetry. Her poems have appeared in *Art Times*, *Paintbrush*, and *Monterey Peninsula Herald*. She is currently revising a novel about Monterey.

Ilea Swinehart is in the eighth grade at Centreville Junior High. She likes playing volleyball and reading. She has one older brother named Jason.

Katrina Tefft likes swimming, reading, and riding. She likes helping, working a little. She loves fruit! Her favorite fruit is strawberries.

Todd Thiel is in the eighth grade and loves to play sports.

Janet Tower is a high school English teacher, wife, mother of twin 13-year-old boys, sister, friend, traveler, reader, lover and player of music, gardener, observer of nature and a joyous member of her extended families. As a reader and writer, she is moved by the pleasure and power of words.

Tiffany L. Troyer is thirteen years old and is entering the eighth grade at Centreville Junior High. She enjoys writing, reading, signing and drawing. She lives with her mom and has one brother and two stepsisters.

Anne Irgens Vandermolen graduated from Denison University with a BA and has an MFA in printmaking from Western Michigan University. She is presently a librarian at St. Joseph Public Library. She is working on a novel and screenplay. She is a member of Sunset Coast Writers. Previously published in *The Blossom Review*.

Bethany Ann Vizthum is 10 years old. She has two sisters and two brothers and her mom and dad. She loves to play soccer and hockey.

Ron Weber is an Associate Member of the Academy of American Poets and has been published in a number of small press and university literary magazines, journals and quarterlies. He has two grown sons and lives with his wife, Connie, on ten acres of the rolling countryside of Southwestern Michigan.

Mary Ann Wehler. Susan Bright, publisher at Plain View Press says of Mary Ann, "This poet has the wisdom of the crone and the energy of the new writer—flowering, exuberant." One of her poems was nominated for a 1998 Pushcart Award.

Lynn Welsch is a seventh grade English teacher at Fennville Middle School. When she's not busy teaching or helping out at the winery, she likes to sing and read. Her favorite place to read? In a lawn chair looking out at the vineyards!

Reneé White was born in and resides in Southwest Michigan and that is the area in which she raised her three children. She is presently teaching at Lake

Michigan Catholic Senior High School and feels a strong love for the state and local community.

Sheri L. Willems has traveled extensively throughout the world and has lived in many rural and isolated areas. She currently lives in Niles with her three children Erica, Kate, and Luther.

Ann Louise Williamson came to Southwest Michigan in 1967. She and Charlie reared their family there. She misses the half inch of sand they had in the bathtubs all summer. Her fun now is *"coaching"* the Whitcomb Writers.

Logan Witt presently is a retired dairy farmer. He also is in the auction business as is one of his sons. This business started in 1957. They do mostly farm and household sales, but have also sold some purebred livestock. He started writing poetry about twenty years ago as a hobby. He has a collection of about forty poems. They are about his life growing up on a family farm. He also have a number of poems based on his life as a Christian and they deal with biblical themes.

Andrew Woolf is 13 years old. His hobbies are skeet shooting, four-wheeling, wrestling, soccer, and football.

Kitty Wunderlin has been teaching twenty-three years. She was the Kalamazoo Farm Bureau Teacher of the Year in 1997 and 1998. She worked in the TCWP Advanced Institute this summer.

Brook Yaw lives in Niles, Michigan.